Building Piece by Peace

Building Piece by Peace

The History of Holland House

Christine Collins

The publishers would like to express their thanks and gratitude to Christine Collins and the staff of Holland House, for their help in preparing this volume.

First published in 1995

Gracewing
Fowler Wright Books
2 Southern Ave, Leominster
Herefordshire HR6 0QF

Gracewing books are distributed

In New Zealand by
Catholic Supplies Ltd
80 Adelaide Road
Wellington
New Zealand

In Australia by
Charles Paine Pty Ltd
8 Ferris Street
North Parramatta
NSW 2151 Australia

In USA by
Morehouse Publishing
PO Box 1321
Harrisburg
PA 17105 USA

In Canada by
Meakin and Associates
Unit 17, 81 Aurega Drive
Nepean, Ontario
KZE 7Y5, Canada

Typesetting by Reesprint, Radley, Oxon, OX14 3AJ
Printed by Progressive Printing

ISBN 0 85244 344 7

Contents

Foreword

by the Bishop of Worcester

I congratulate Holland House and all its friends on the fiftieth anniversary of the holding of the first retreat in what was known as *The Old House*. This history of the house is a fitting contribution to the celebrations. It tells the story of a house which was and is a gift to the Church.

The story is told with great affection. To read it is a heart-warming experience. From the time when the house grew out of a series of cottages to the present day when it is a laity centre with an ecumenical and a European character, Holland House has been loved. G.K. Chesterton said that before a thing can be lovely it has got to be loved. The story of the house bears out the truth of Chesterton's dictum.

Mrs Holland must be rejoicing at the way the story has unfolded. The description of the way furniture and fittings were acquired at sales or just by kind gifts from near and far is reminiscent of the days when the Church was less bureaucratic than it is today. How good it was that the growing retreat house and conference centre was rescued from a plethora of notices more appropriate for an Edwardian reform school! Thankfully, Holland House is marvellously non-institutional.

It would not be wise to mention names for fear of missing out some who played an important part in the story. However, we have to acknowledge the courage and foresight of all the Trustees who prevented the house from becoming lost for ever to the Diocese of Worcester and the Church of England. Indeed, it has since become a centre treasured by all denominations.

Now it is a laity centre run by a devoted and competent team doing much each day beyond the call of duty. 'Laity centre' to me means a place where Christian faith is learned and absorbed within the culture it has inspired and imbued. Many people discover Christian faith, not by trying to look straight at the bright white light of Christ, but by taking in these less blinding but many-coloured reflecting surfaces, both in history and in contemporary culture.

May Holland House flourish for many more decades to the great advantage of future generations.

+ Philip Worcester

Introduction

When I was first asked to write the history of Holland House, I soon realised that I had a fascinating task which would inevitably fall into two natural areas. The first of these was of course the history of the house, a building dating as far as we can tell from the late sixteenth, or early seventeenth century. The second was its period of change and development throughout its fifty years as a house for peaceful retreat and Christian spirituality and friendship, within a wide-ranging sphere of activities and interests.

The early history of the house before the 1860s is undocumented, as it formed part of a group of labourers' cottages under various ownership. There are some documents which show the sale and purchase of different items from this group in the 1860s, but they are not always easily identifiable as specific cottages. The earliest document, a deed of conveyance, that can be positively identified as belonging to a part of what is now Holland House is dated September 1865.

In so far as the more recent history is concerned, that of the past fifty years, I have had great delight in meeting people who have known the house throughout this period, first when it was known as *The Old House* and later when it was given the name of its owner and generous benefactor.

I regret that I have only known Holland House for the past five or six years, but during this time I have come to know it well and have benefited greatly from all that it has to offer.

Acknowledgements

I would like to express my appreciation of all the help that I
have been given in writing this history from the Warden Peter
Middlemiss and the Deputy Warden William Swabey, the Rt
Revd Kenneth Woollcombe former Bishop of Oxford, the
Ven. Canon Peter and Lady Alethea Eliot, the Diocesan
Registrar M.G. Huskinson, Mrs. Diana Beswick (formerly
Diana Day), Miss Evelyn James, Mrs Ida Baker (formerly Ida
Bloomfield), Mrs Gwendoline Blizard and her daughter
Mamie, and many others who have written to me with
personal reminiscences; in particular Gladys Mayes whose
memories of the early post-war days and on into the sixties
were so particularly vivid.

The illustrations in this book have been drawn by Jean
Gray and Deputy Warden William Swabey.

For expertise in describing and identifying aspects of old
buildings I am particularly indebted to Derek Watson, whose
great interest in this subject has made him a most valuable
source of information. The interest and help of all these
friends of Holland House has been a great inspiration and
encouragement in writing this history.

1

The Village of Cropthorne

The Domesday Record of 1086 shows CROPETORN to have been the name of the eleventh-century village we now know as Cropthorne, but an even earlier chronicle, (Birch, *Cartularium Saxonicum*) records that in the year 708 the area was known as CROPPENPORN(E). *Place Names of Worcestershire* (Vol. 4) lists the name of the village as CROPPONTHORNE in the eighth century and CROPPANHORNE in the ninth century. The same work gives the spelling as CROPPE-THORNE by the twelfth century and by 1305 the Calendar of patent roles also records the name as CROPPETHORNE.

The variations in the dates and spellings should give no concern since few at that time could write and those who were literate would spell phonetically. This combined with differing pronunciation could, and often did, produce wide variations in place and personal names. The *Victoria County History* for Worcester (Vol. 3) also suggests that the name may derive from an otherwise unknown person with the nickname of Croppa which may have derived from the Old English Cropp or sprout bunch. This is mainly speculation but certainly in 1428 the name was still spelt as it had been over one hundred years earlier.

However the Rev. George Mills in a work published in 1890 *The Parishes of the Diocese of Worcester* considers that the derivation is Cropt — a field and Horne — a corner. Mills also suggests that in the year 786 Offa, King of Mercia

1

(757–796), gave the area to the Church of Worcester. The area was not, in this period, remote from royal interest, since the centre for the exercise of the King's power was nearby Winchcombe. There is an interesting story or legend regarding this gift. Until the Reformation the Diocese of Worcester covered a very wide area from Warwickshire to Bristol. Within this large Diocese were some eighteen manors which hosted the Bishop on his episcopal visits. For many centuries the Bishops had a residence at Fladbury and it is said that in 780 Tilhere, the then Bishop, entertained Offa, King of Mercia and builder of the great dyke, to a truly royal banquet. As a reward for this hospitality Offa granted to the Bishop and his Diocese the village of Cropthorne and other lands. Included with this generous gift was a bible with clasps of gold. It is also believed that there was a royal hunting lodge at Cropthorn in Saxon times. Two other royal visits have been made to the village, one in 1291 by Edward I and Charles I in 1644.

The Church of St Michael in Cropthorne dates from before the Norman Conquest. The Domesday Record shows that the Priory of Worcester provided a priest for Cropthorne in 1086. The earliest part of the present building, the base of the chancel arch, dates from about 1100 AD. The church contains an Anglo-Saxon cross, which once rested on a window ledge in the Lady Chapel, but more recently has been near the north door. This cross, thought to date from 800 AD, was displayed by the British Museum in an exhibition mounted in 1992 entitled *Anglo-Saxon England*.

The Domesday Record has the following entry for Cropthorne:

Cropetorn: Worcester Church, Mill. 20 sticks of eels.

The 'twenty sticks of eels' would have been the yearly rent paid for the mill, 20 sticks being 500 eels. Eels are still to be found in the Avon, where it flows past the lower slopes of the gardens of what is now Holland House.

Whatever the derivation of the name, the present-day village of Cropthorne is still a small and very attractive place, set in the Vale of Evesham and little changed from the late nineteenth and early part of the twentieth century. Several of the attractive houses and cottages are thatched and Cropthorne Court, once the home of the Squire Francis Dermot Holland is still in private occupation. Since the dissolution of the monasteries, the Lords of the Manor of Cropthorne have been the Dean and Chapter of Worcester Cathedral.

Cropthorne lies just off the Pershore to Evesham Road, with Holland House occupying a prominent position in the main street. The house, a grade-two listed building, probably dates in part from the seventeenth century or the late sixteenth century although over the years it has been very much altered and enlarged.

The House and its Earlier Development

The house which, together with its gardens, is now known as Holland House was originally a collection of several smaller properties, cottages, orchards and outbuildings which over a period of years were brought under one ownership, mainly by Sir William Lawson Tait, a surgeon practising at that time in Birmingham, and then by Henry Howard Avery, a member of the Birmingham firm of the same name, manufacturers of weighing scales.

It would appear that Sir William Tait lived in *The Den*, as he called it, for a comparatively short time, or maybe used it as a summer retreat, since only three years after buying it he leased it to Avery. Tait bought the property in 1891 from an Allen Lankaster Haynes of Evesham for the sum of £500. From the conveyance documents it would appear that he was buying the cottages that formed the basis of Holland House and some of the top area of the garden; the property was then known as *Home Orchard*. Later the same year he bought an unnamed orchard from the then Squire of Cropthorne,

Francis Dermot Holland. For this piece of orchard land he paid £150.

In 1893 Sir William bought a part of Butcher's Orchard from Francis Holland; this piece of land would appear to have been included in what is now the garden of Holland House.

Although Sir William was obviously adding to the property in so far as the land was concerned, it would appear that he was also making considerable changes to the buildings or cottages. What had been described as a tenement or messuage with outbuildings and land worth a total of £500 in 1891, had by the year 1894 become known as *The Den* and was leased to a Samuel Henry Keeling for a period of seven years.

The schedule for the lease of *The Den* shows by this time a house of some size and status, having at least five bedrooms, one with a wash-basin plumbed in (described in the document as Mrs Tait's bedroom), one bathroom, together with water closets both upstairs and downstairs, high standards for the period. Accommodation also included a drawing room, dining room and morning room. It is interesting to note that a bell indicator, for calling servants to a particular room and apparently dating from well before 1920, is still in position in the passage at the entrance to the present kitchens. The indicator lists six bedrooms, night and day nurseries as well as drawing room, dining room and study and was in all probability installed by Howard Avery after he had enlarged and altered the property. By 1894 Sir William had also installed a windmill on the roof of the coach house and stables. This windmill would seem to have been part of an innovative sewerage system installed by Sir William, and was an extraordinary-looking contraption standing on the roof, supported by two platforms on angled supports. From early photographs it would seem to have been of some considerable height. In the 1894 letting schedule of the house the description is of:

A windmill by 'Pontifex and Wood' (as) fixed on stables with two platforms and semi-rotary pump by Evans, an endless chain sewage pump by Parker and Winder.

(This pump probably brought water from the river to the house for domestic use, being replaced by the contraption remembered by Ida Bloomfield in the 1920s.) Neighbouring properties show a variety of methods of dealing with sewage and drainage in the same period. The dynamics of obtaining fresh water, and dispersing waste were common to all properties in that part of the village, due to the lie of the land and long slope to the river. Several houses had their own water supply via a well within the garden or grounds.

Samuel Keeling did not complete the seven years of his lease, the reason for this is not documented; in 1898 Sir William leased the house to Henry Howard Avery, on an annual basis at a rent of £65. The schedule for the lease was the same as that for the lease to Keeling, there would seem to have been no material alterations to the property. There is no further mention of Sir William Lawson Tait in the archive material relating to the house, although there is a copy of a letter from Somerset House confirming that there was no duty payable on the death of a *Robert* Lawson Tait, who died on 13th September 1899. Since 1899 is thought to be the year in which Sir *William* Tait died, it is possible that the letter contains an inaccuracy as to the Christian name, or could Robert have been the principal inheritor of Sir William's estate, unfortunately dying in the same year? It seems a strange coincidence if this is the case.

Avery's Ownership

It would appear, although there are no documents to substantiate this, that at some time between 1898 and 1903 Avery became the owner rather than the lessee of The Den, since he remained living there, buying adjoining land and cottages to enlarge the property.

In June 1903 Avery bought from a Mrs Elizabeth Hanlin (née Harris) 'three messuages at Cropthorne, for the sum of £150'. There is no plan shown on the conveyance, but the

cottages were possibly three cottages on Kennel Bank, adjoining land belonging to *The Den* and *The Taylors*. In October
of the following year Avery was to buy from George Harris
the property known as *The Taylors*. From a simple plan and
description accompanying the deed of conveyance The Tay-
lors would appear to be orchard, garden, cottage buildings
and yard, most of which now forms the lower part of Holland
House gardens. The land was described in the deed as being
under cultivation as orchard and pasture; the price for the
land and buildings, totalling just over an acre, was £700.

In January 1913 Avery was able to buy 54½ square yards
of Vicarage land from the church. The conveyance agreeing
to this sale is in the possession of the Worcester Diocesan
Registrar, and is a fascinating document since it contains the
signatures and seals of the then Archbishop of Canterbury,
Randall Thomas Davidson, and Huyshe Wolcott Yeatman
Biggs, Bishop of Worcester. It would appear that this piece
of land was required for the purpose of enlarging the house
still further by adding a timber-framed building which is the
existing two-storey kitchen wing, main entrance hall and
lounge. The development at the rear required the demoli-
tion of the coach house and stables together with the windmill. This work was certainly completed by 1920, since the
outline plan on the conveyance to Mrs Holland clearly shows
that the long coach house and stables are no longer in
existence, and the house has been enlarged right up to the
new boundary.

One of the frustrations of working on the history of Holland House, as a building, is the total lack of plans belonging
to this period of its development. The larger part of the
house must be post-1880, yet despite exhaustive searches no
architect's plans or sketches, no working drawings of any sort
have been discovered. The only way in which any clue can
be obtained, apart from written descriptions on documents
is from the blocked outline of buildings on deeds of convey-

ance and the schedule drawn up on the occasion of the first letting to Keeling.

There is a gable in the original house which is thought to have been built or enlarged by Avery, since the initials H.H.A. and the date 1904 are boldly carved on the bressumer of the left-hand gable of the three main gables of the house. On the cill of the ground-floor window of the same gable is incised the name Drinkwater Butt FRPS and also the date 1904. There has been much speculation as to who Drinkwater Butt was. Could he have been the architect of the enlarged gable, was the name by way of being a joke, a play on words? Enquiries show that there was a Fellow of the Royal Photographic Society in 1895 listed as Drinkwater Butt, maybe he had parents with a warped sense of humour, or perhaps he devised for himself a rather unforgettable professional name. There was also an Architect living in Birmingham in 1914 called Charles Frederick Butt. According to the Royal Institute of British Architect records he was an associate in 1913, becoming a Fellow in 1929. He would appear to have been rather young in 1904 to have designed the gable. However if, as suggested by an article in *The Ideal Home* or similar magazine dated some time prior to 1915, the gable is actually of a later date, this would seem to be possible. The pages taken from this magazine have a photograph showing a corner of the house, the caption reading:

> The Den, Cropthorne, showing the new gable, sunk garden and sundial.

This article and caption would seem to suggest that the gable was built or enlarged somewhere between 1911 and 1913, the name Drinkwater Butt and 1904 relating to something other than the construction or alteration of the gable or house. Unfortunately the apparent timescale of ownership given in the article seem to tie in with neither the pictures accompanying the text nor the dates we have documented. Regrettably the magazine article is not dated, but, from the trace of the windmill visible, it was obviously before 1915.

All we do know for sure is that, whoever he was and for whatever reason, his name and the date 1904 were added, albeit somewhat casually as to execution, along with that of the owner of the house, on the new gable. The gable in question extended the room that is now part of the dining room, overlooking the paved sunken garden.

The Garden

This brings us to the garden, which it has been suggested was designed by Sir Edwin Lutyens. There is no proof of this, although in some correspondence in June 1979 Mrs Margaret Richardson, Deputy Curator of The British Architectural Library, refers to this possibility. Apparently in Butler's publication *The Architecture of Sir William Lutyens* he notes for the year 1900 'Garden at the Den, Pershore for Mr H. Avery'. Secondly Lutyens writing to his wife on 15th April 1901 told her that a Mr Avery of Birmingham had written to the magazine *Country Life* requesting the name of an architect to '... do a garden sloping down to a river' (RIBA MS Collection). It is possible therefore that he did have at least some influence on the design of the garden even if he did not plan and carry out the design in its entirety. Regrettably again no plans or drawings exist, so it is not possible to make any positive claims. One thing does seem fairly certain and that is that the sundial was after a design by Lutyens, with the words 'I number none but sunny hours' and it can clearly be seen from early photographs that the sunken garden, morain and water gardens were designed and built to a high standard. The gardens included a tennis lawn and dovecot together with many borders and a considerable amount of decorative trellis work. Other magazine photographs of the paved and sunken gardens taken before 1920 are still easily recognisable as the gardens of today, especially where they are near the house, and many of the low box hedges used as edging to paths and borders are still as originally planted.

The article in the magazine, which refers to the Averys by name, would seem to have been published between 1917 and 1919, since by 1920, following the death of Eileen their young daughter aged about six, the Averys had sold the property to Mrs Amy Elizabeth Holland. The photographs used to illustrate the article show a garden in full summer flowering, probably mid to late June. The beautiful gardens were certainly created during the time H.H. Avery owned the house. It is Avery who is recorded as having bought parcels of land and orchard towards the river and also adjoining Kennel Bank, and who is then described in the article a having set about clearing parts of the old orchard to give views across the valley of the Avon and also of course opening up the gardens to give the present wide views with lawns sloping down to the river.

Other photographs of the village of Cropthorne may be seen in a fascinating book of photographs entitled *Cropthorne Camera of Minnie Holland*. Although published only fairly recently (text dated 1978), the photographs were taken between 1894 and 1905 by Miss Minnie Holland, daughter of Francis Dermot Holland, Squire of the Village and owner of Cropthorne Court. The photographs also show family groups of the Holland family, and houses and cottages, often with local residents standing nearby. These photographs were discovered as a collection of glass negatives in an antique shop in Plymouth by C.D. and G.H. Webb a husband and wife who had no connection with this part of the world, but, by printing the negatives and discovering the words 'Cropthorne Post Office' visible in one of the prints, finally traced the village. They stayed with Mrs Knowles at her Guest House while they identified all the photographs and, with the help of Mrs. Cornell, were able to name not only cottages and houses but the various people also in the photographs. Unfortunately there were no photographs of the main house, *The Den*, which is a pity, as it is probable that during the period of these photographs many of the major changes were taking place. There are however, in the context of Kennel Corner, photographs of parts of Kennel Bank and the cottages in the lane, some of which are still there, although several were removed during all the changes to Holland House and its grounds .

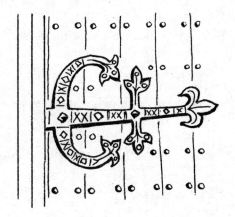

2

Mrs Amy Elizabeth Holland

On 11th November 1920 Mrs Amy Elizabeth Holland of *The Court House*, Birlingham, near Pershore, became the owner of *The Den* which she bought from H.H. Avery who had lived in it since 1898 although he had leased it from Sir William Tait for at least the first year of his occupancy. Ownership probably dating as already suggested from about 1900. Mrs Holland was the widow of Colonel Ellis Holland RA the younger son of Francis Dermot Holland of Cropthorne Court.

Mrs Holland paid £6,400 for the property described as *The Den* and four cottages adjoining. The deed of conveyance shows a plan in outline of the house now known as Holland House together with cottages fronting Kennel Bank. It is this plan that shows a residential wing where the long narrow stable building had been, having been either totally demolished or partially incorporated into the new wing. It is difficult to be sure at what point the house ceased to be known as *The Den* and became *The Old House*. One thing is certain: Mrs. Holland did not immediately change the name, since she bought a piece of Glebe land in May 1921 and the house is still described in the conveyance as *The Den*. This piece of land gave her good access to the 'new wing' built by Avery. (It should perhaps be noted that the name *The Den* now applies to a house in the grounds on Kennel Corner.)

As has already been mentioned, precise dating of the original cottages is not possible, although Derek Watson, a resident of Cropthorne — who takes a scholarly interest in old buildings and has made a personal study of architectural history — believes the oldest section to date from a period between 1580 and 1620. He is able to say with some certainty that the cross-wing is the oldest part of the building, the timber framing being similar to that of several other Crop-thorne houses, the dimensions of the gable of the cross-wing, *c.* 15 feet across, being the same as a house known as *Perseus* nearby. From this cross-wing a two- or three-bay timber-framed building extended for about 37 feet north-east. To quote Derek Watson:

> The original building could have therefore been of two or three bays with a depth of *c.* 17 feet, which is standard for such timber-framed houses.

During the enlargement of the house, the rear wall, onto the garden, would have been removed, allowing an extension some ten or eleven feet to the back of the house. This addition is clearly seen in the dining room, where two up-rights divide the later section of the room from the original, the later part forming a bay. There are two carved spandrels between these uprights, one has a coat of arms, the other the date 1636 and the initials H.W. and a small cross. It would seem that these were at no time part of the original cottages, the workmanship being of much too high a quality for what would at that time have been workmen's cottages. The presence of a coat of arms, not identified, would also suggest that they were in all probability obtained by Sir William as decoration for the supports, helping to give the impression of a shallow archway into the newer area of the dining room. It is of course perfectly possible that either Howard Avery or Mrs Elizabeth Holland decided to install the carvings as a way of enhancing the room. The spandrels are carved on only one face, suggesting that they were originally designed for use against another upright surface rather than free-standing as in their present position. They were possibly part of a decorative overmantel or door arch. Unfortunately we not

only do not know who placed them in the dining room, we
have no idea of their origin, only that they have obviously
come from a building of some quality.

Another rather puzzling aspect of some of the timbers
visible at the library end of the dining room are joists running
longitudinally from the cross-wing, ending abruptly above
the south-west wall of the dining room. Derek Watson is
unable to say with certainty whether these were left as found
by the architect who designed the timber-framed extension.
The impression given is of the exterior end of a building
being incorporated within an interior.

The original area of the dining room has a recessed fireplace decorated with Delft-ware tiles (probably Dutch rather
than English Delft), the tiles and fire grate or basket were of
course added when the fireplace was converted, probably
during Avery's ownership. Above the present fireplace is a
large chimney, visible through a small metal trap, showing
that this now somewhat enclosed sub-area was also the
original much larger and more open fireplace.

In the cloakroom on the ground floor is a washbasin that
would seem to date from the plumbing and sanitary arrange-
ments installed by Sir William or at the latest by Howard
Avery soon after he took possession of the house. It is a quite
magnificent arrangement being a large corner basin fitted
with brass taps and patent 'plunger' contraption with 'claw'-
shaped base, presumably to prevent foreign bodies from
entering the drain pipe, and a plug to retain the water.
Manufactured by Doulton, it would appear to date from the
turn of the century.

Examination of the interior of the roof structure confirms
not only that the greater part of Holland House as it now
exists is post-1880, but that a considerable area of the 'new
house' is post-1904 as there are (reinforced metal) beams in
areas of the roof timbering.

Memories of 1920–1925

Memories of those who lived at the *Old House* during the time of Mrs Holland's ownership, but prior to its becoming a retreat house, are of necessity few. Mrs Muriel Carter (née Houghton) has still some very clear girlhood memories of those far-off days. In 1936, when she was nine years old, she moved with her family to Cropthorne. Mrs Carter well remembers as a girl of ten or eleven helping to scrub the stone flags of the house, and a few years later being interviewed by Mrs Holland for her first job. This interview took place in 1941 and was for a place in service at Bricklehampton Hall. No doubt her childhood willingness to help with the scrubbing of stone floors stood her in good stead, as she obtained the post. At about this time Mrs Holland had two maids at the *Old House*, Milly Robbins and Mrs Joan Shotter. The most vivid memories of the *Old House* are surely held by Mrs Ida Alice Baker (née Bloomfield) whose father Olaf Bloomfield was Chauffeur to Colonel and Mrs Holland when they lived in Ipswich, moving with them first to Birlingham and then Cropthorne. Ida, her older sister Hilda Maud, and her younger sister Phyllis, were young children when they moved to Cropthorne.

Ida remembered the fun she and her friends had when, not long after moving in, Mrs Holland went to Canada for some three months. The Bakers moved from their cottage in the grounds into the house. Ida remembered how:

> All the silver was taken to the bank and we 'lived in' to look after the house. We used to play lovely games on the long landing upstairs, there were such wonderful corners to hide in.

The visit that Mrs Holland made to Canada was probably inspired by a friend who wanted to build a church in that country (eventually built at McCready, Manitoba). Mrs Holland and another friend, a Mrs Christie, were at that time members of the Oxford Movement, an Anglo-Catholic organisation. It is very likely that through this group and, it is believed, her friendship with Mrs Christie, that Mrs Holland was inspired at a later date to give her home as a retreat house to the Diocese of Worcester.

Gladys Mayes was to recall a 'friend who gave annual lantern lectures about her work in Canada'. This friend travelled with a caravan in the remote region of north-west Canada where she started Sunday-schools and women's groups. When back in this country, she was always raising funds for this work which had enabled her to build a church in Canada in the early 1930s. Cropthorne gave a great deal towards this fund, and the church at McCready, Manitoba, was named St Michael and all Angels after Cropthorne's parish church. Gladys Mayes also remembered how:

> At St Andrew's-tide Mrs Holland liked to have a sale of work in the *Old House*, the proceeds going to missionary work. There were flowers and plants from her garden and things she had made and friends had given. On one occasion there were some paintings that a friend had done, mostly of the *Old House* and the village.

It is very probable that this 'missionary work' was the work her friend was busy with in north-west Canada. There is a watercolour of the Canadian church of St Michael in Cropthorne church. This watercolour is signed F.H. White or Waite (1933) and is believed to have been painted by the same friend who had done so much to enable the church to be built.

It is interesting to note that at about the same period as Mrs. Holland was giving her home to the Diocese as a retreat house, a Miss Amy Buller was launching another 'Christian-minded' house, elsewhere in England. Amy Buller was a graduate of Birkbeck College before the First World War and had travelled extensively in Germany between the wars, she was therefore particularly dismayed:

> ... to find how easily people who had graduated through the great German universities had been seduced by the brutal

philosophy of Nazism... [and] the suppression of free speech
that had made this possible.

Even before the war, Miss Buller had conceived the idea of
founding (or re-founding) residential Christian centres. In
particular, she wanted, with Royal approval, to re-found the
Royal Foundation of St Katherine in London, a medieval
charitable institution, and enable it to return as near as
possible to its original site, in the Docklands. She also conceived the idea of a 'college', not attached to any university,
where teachers and students could come in order to discuss
'great issues of the day'. The outbreak of the Second World
War caused her plans to be postponed, although during the
war her considerable knowledge of Germany led her to write
an important book, *Darkness Over Germany* (1943) which came
to the notice of the then Queen Elizabeth, now the Queen
Mother. In 1947 Queen Elizabeth and King George approved
the removal of the Royal Foundation of St Katherine to the
East End once more, where it began to convert a property
into a retreat house and conference centre that is still flour-
ishing today, near the Docklands Light Railway. The King
and Queen also granted the Foundation a second centre at
Cumberland Lodge, a former royal residence in Windsor
Great Park, which still operates as a conference centre today.

Neither were such initiatives limited to this country. At
the same time in Germany, a similar inspiration in the wake
of the war led a Lutheran pastor, Eberhard Müller, to estab-
lish the first of the German Church Academies. Their aim
paralleled that of Amy Butler — to create centres where
issues could be discussed openly, so that the Nazi experience
could not be repeated. Today there are over forty Protestant
and Catholic Academies in Germany alone, with a growing
number of various denominations across the world, and most
notably in recent years in Eastern European countries. For
this reason Holland House has been, since 1993, a member
of the European Association of Academies and Laity Centres.

Yet English centres also differ from those in other parts of Europe by their emphasis on running retreats.

It is perfectly feasible that the two women, Mrs Holland and Miss Buller were known to each other through the Oxford Movement, or that Mrs Holland had been inspired by *Darkness Over Germany*. It is in any case interesting to note that two independent women should be embarking on such similar projects more or less simultaneously.

During those earlier years Mrs Holland maintained a staff of six, quite usual for a house of the size and prestige of the *Old House* at that time. The staff consisted of the chauffeur Mr Bloomfield, Mr Hyde the head gardener, an under-gardener and three maids.

One of the aspects of the house that Ida particularly remembers was a 'very noisy contraption outside the kitchen door'. This was a mechanical water pump of some type that brought water to the house either from the river for house-hold use, or from a well which was known to be near the back door. This was probably a replacement for the 'windmill' type installation previously listed in the Tait schedule as having been situated on the roof. As far as can be ascertained, this 'windmill' was removed by 1915, as Mrs Gwendoline Blizard, who has lived in the village since then, has no memory of it at all. When shown photographs of the house which included the 'windmill', she was quite certain that it was no longer there in 1915. 'We lived in a cottage opposite the house, and I could never have missed that.' This is regrettably the nearest it has been possible to date the removal of this quite incredible contraption.

Although Mrs Holland had a reputation over many years for being very 'careful' with her money, which had come from the Lancashire cotton industry, Ida remembers one particular act of generosity to her father while they were still in Ipswich. It was during the Great War, and Ida still has the letter dated 1915 written to her father, hoping all was well with him and telling him that a hamper had been despatched to him from Harrods, in the hope that it would bring him a few comforts.

After the war and Olaf Bloomfield's return to England, he continued his employment with Colonel and Mrs Holland, moving with them to Worcestershire, where they went first to Birlingham. Once they had moved to Cropthorne, Olaf became a member of the church choir and was later appointed a Churchwarden.

Ida clearly remembers the winter of 1927 when there was severe flooding and the milk had to be delivered from Pattys Farm, which is situated just at the foot of the hill, by rowing boat. Before the worst of the floods, there had been such severe cold that Olaf Bloomfield was able to skate across flooded fields from Cropthorne to Fladbury. Pattys Farm, then owned by the Meakins, is also renowned as a house were John Wesley preached. The story goes that such were the crowds who wanted to hear the great preacher that in true Biblical fashion a hole was knocked through a ceiling so that those crowded into the upper part of the house could also hear John Wesley's words.

The weather also played an important part in the May Day celebrations for the children of the village. A fine sunny day for the first of May meant that the Maypole dance, the traditional plaiting of the ribbons hung from the top of the Maypole, and all the accompanying celebrations and dressing up could be enjoyed to the full. In the early years of her residence at the *Old House*, Mrs Holland would invite the dancers to bring the Maypole and perform their traditional dances on the top lawn of the *Old House*. In one photograph of the children, Ida's younger sister Phyllis, then aged eight, can clearly be seen. Those were very patriotic days, with much waving of the Union Jack and blowing of miniature trumpets. The girls wore garlands of flowers and the boys dressed in the costumes of the Empire.

3

The First Meetings

The earliest meetings held at *The Old House* (as Holland House would be known until 1975) were during 1944 when Miss Joan Harcombe gave training classes for those teaching in Sunday schools. These were held in the dining room, and Joan Harcombe remembers how everyone enjoyed gathering around the log fire in the deep fireplace. It was Mrs Holland's custom to join the group for part of the evening, as she was still living in the house until the summer of 1946.

The very first retreat was held in October 1945. It consisted of a group from St Stephen's Church, Redditch, and was led by the Vicar's wife, Mrs Bradley. The retreat was directed by Father Long. Again one of the abiding memories that those who attended the retreat took away with them was the beauty of the gardens. In 1944 Miss Monica James had returned to England from her work in Africa, and through a mutual friend was approached by Mrs Holland to help her in the work of creating a retreat centre in Cropthorne. An early and major problem was the need for more furniture, and she recalls Mrs Holland giving her money, the use of her car, and some precious petrol which was still rationed, so that she could travel to auction sales throughout the county trying to buy furniture. At that time new furniture was only available to those who had a particular need, for instance newly-weds or those who had lost their homes in the war. They would be provided with special 'dockets' enabling them to buy what

19

the government officially designated 'Utility furniture' and which was the only furniture allowed to be manufactured at that time. All secondhand furniture was therefore at a premium, and Monica James well remembers her feelings on being continually 'pipped at the post' by antique dealers from places such as Broadway.

These shortages meant using a considerable amount of ingenuity, and converting items of furniture to uses other than those for which they had been designed. One ingenious conversion or change of use was when they turned a chest of drawers back to front to form the basis of the altar for the chapel. The black cotton material used to 'black-out' windows during the war was everywhere and put to many uses other than its original purpose. It was quite good-quality soft cotton and, with the use of bright embroidery, cotton and *appliqué* patterns could be adapted for many uses including skirts and blouses.

Soon groups of people were coming to the house for more than just the training classes, but were beginning to gather for prayer and discussion. Soon some of the people taking part were staying overnight or longer. In 1945 a series of retreats was held for Sunday-school teachers. Organised by Miss Joan Harcombe these retreats, which were to be the first of many, took place shortly after a Warden was first appointed to help run the house as a centre for Christian spirituality.

These early retreats took the form of a devotional weekend, during which silence was kept all the time, a new concept for many of those attending. One of the early retreatants discussing them many years later spoke of her astonishment at finding a veil laid out on her bed. This was to be worn over her head, 'like a girl in a convent'. Miss Harcombe also ran 'A School of Prayer' for young people, when silence was kept from after Compline in the evening until after breakfast the next morning. During fine weather, talks and discussions often took place in the gardens, usually in the rose garden: this outdoor life added to the joy of the retreats, especially for those living in towns and cities.

At that time the chapel was in what is now the library and, although it was a lovely room for devotions, all who used it mention one particular distraction. Directly outside the window in the front of the house, across the very narrow strip of garden was a bus stop. During the summer, when windows were often wide open, there was the continual sound of chattering and laughter as people waited for transport. Despite the distractions, Gwendoline Blizard still thinks of that room as perfect for a chapel, and only recently remarked how much she had enjoyed polishing the beautiful wood floor, and how peaceful the room had always been.

In the summer of 1946 Mrs Holland moved across the road to *Pound House* which had recently become vacant. It was probably at about this time that Mrs Holland decided on the future of the house as a diocesan retreat centre. Colonel and Mrs Holland having no children, there were no immediate heirs to whom the house should be left. The use of the *Old House* as a meeting place for Christian discussion and prayer was growing and seemed to be fulfilling a considerable need.

Bishop William Cash of the Worcester Diocese was approached as to whether he would or could take the house under the auspices of the Diocese as a retreat house. Much as Bishop Cash would have liked the Diocese to have accepted this offer, he felt unable to, since the running costs would have been more than it could have afforded. The outcome was that Mrs Holland asked the Bishop to permit the use of the house as a retreat centre, guaranteeing that she would be responsible for the financial aspects of the venture. This of course the Bishop was only to happy to do. The *Old House* thus became a Retreat and Conference Centre attached to the Diocese of Worcester. In the future, the Bishop was to use the house frequently, particularly for groups of visiting clergy.

By the autumn of 1946, Mrs Holland was beginning to realise that the considerable use to which the house was now being put was really becoming more than she could cope with. Living in *Pound House* and looking after the guests in the *Old House*, together with all the correspondence and administrative work was not really practicable. It was really necessary to have someone living in the house and devoting all her time and energies to its success.

The outcome of this decision was that in October 1946 Deaconess Sybil Mayes was licensed by the Bishop as the first Warden of the Old House, her salary to be paid by the Diocese. Even so, the work of the house was growing, and it was fairly obvious that more help was necessary on the domestic-management side. It was hoped that Sybil's sister Gladys would be able to become part of the venture that same year, but unfortunately due to illness she was not able to do this straight away. However, Deaconess Mayes had a friend who was able to fill in until the following March, when Gladys was able to join her sister and take up her new rôle at the *Old House*. The two sisters were to remain in Cropthorne until ill-health forced Sybil into retirement in 1961.

Early Days and Practical Difficulties

The winter of 1947 was one that all those who experienced it are unlikely to forget. Heavy snowfalls all over the country, combined with hard frosts, made life very difficult in town and country. To add to the problems of the weather, there were still severe shortages of almost all day-to-day necessities including food and fuel, even though it was two years since the end of the Second World War. All forms of fossil fuel were in short supply or rationed, and coal became even more difficult to obtain that winter, owing to a long-lasting strike by the nation's coalminers.

Electricity was cut off at regular periods throughout the 24 hours, although this made little difference to Cropthorne, as the village was not on the national grid. For people living in and around the village the main problem was shortage of fuel for those who operated their own generators. A stock of candles was a necessity, as were oil lamps to take over in case of electricity failure. Radio broadcasting was strictly regulated to a few hours a day. (Limited television transmission was only just beginning again after the war.) All these problems increased the sense of isolation in rural areas like Cropthorne. Transport was made difficult by lack of petrol and by the appalling weather conditions, supplies were frequently unable to reach the villages and houses cut off by the deep snow.

However, just as Gladys Mayes arrived to join her sister in March of that year, the thaw had begun. Once again the low-lying areas along the river Avon around Pershore, Evesham and Tewkesbury were flooded, and the village of Cropthorne was completely cut off. This meant that several groups planning to come to the *Old House* had their bookings cancelled. Although this seemed a misfortune to everyone concerned at the time, it had the advantage of enabling Gladys to take stock, both literally and metaphorically.

The floods gave both the Deaconess and her sister a breathing space in which they were able to make plans for the future. It had become clear that the reputation of the *Old House* as a place of Christian retreat and prayer was growing, and practical plans and decisions had to be made. It was obviously necessary to take very careful note of what they had in the way of such very basic items as bed-linen, furnishings and household equipment. Mrs Holland had very generously left a good stock cupboard at the house, but it was still a time of severe rationing after the war. In fact in some respects rationing was more difficult than it had been during the war, with many vital necessities being strictly limited. In Gladys's own words she describes it as '... a very sparse household, there were not enough sheets, pillowcases and towels for more than twelve people, which made it impossible for a quick turnover'. It was therefore decided to ask guests staying at the house overnight to bring their own sheets, pillow cases and towels.

All such items were still rationed, with 'Clothing Coupons' being required for the purchase of household linen as well as clothes. Some time later it was possible to obtain 'army surplus' blankets and other items; they were certainly not glamorous but eminently serviceable. Rationing made feeding the visitors difficult, as anyone staying overnight with meals provided had to surrender food coupons, all of which had to be accounted for and the meals taken recorded. The *Old House* was very fortunate in having an excellent kitchen garden, and the fruit and vegetables that this supplied made feeding the guests a lot simpler, as all such supplies were exempt from any of the rules regarding rationing. A house cow would have been a great advantage to the house and its guests, since Gladys remembers the problems of making three pints of milk (less than one and three-quarter litres) per day suffice for twenty people. At this time Mrs Holland kept some dearly loved hens at the bottom of the orchard area of the garden, but whether these would have been of sufficient quantity to help in feeding the guests is not recorded. One memory regarding the hens does come from Monica James, who was one of the very early post-war helpers at the retreat house. She recalls very vividly how after Church Service on Sunday Mrs Holland would present them with their weekly ration of one egg apiece.

Those early visitors to the *Old House* would experience great changes if they were to visit Holland House now. They would find not only the extensive new modern buildings, not only the plentiful and delicious food with which they would be served, with no requirements to sacrifice their own rations. They would also discover that drinking water is no longer pumped from the pump in the kitchen and then filtered, nor the water for baths and washing pumped from the river. There are no longer problems with the electricity supply, as there were in the days before the village was connected to the national grid. Like the Old House, the entire village of Cropthorne in 1947 had no mains water nor main drainage. There were only two bathrooms in those early days, so, with all this to contend with, daily baths were not encouraged! Visitors did not have plumbed-in washing facilities in their rooms, but used the old-fashioned method of a Victorian or Edwardian style washstand, with basin and large matching water jug. It was also necessary to have drinking water, changed daily and placed ready in a carafe in every room, no quick turn of the tap if you were thirsty in the night.

The *Old House* was able to accommodate sixteen overnight visitors, some sharing rooms, so it can be seen that there was a considerable amount of work to be done whenever one group left and another was due to arrive. A great deal of help was provided by one or two women from the village, who cleaned bedrooms and saw to the refilling of those water carafes. This last duty was one that obviously featured large in the day's work, as Gladys mentioned it several times when reminiscing about the early days at the *Old House*. Other people helped with the washing-up after the meals, as this was all done by hand in those days.

This help from people living in the village created a growing relationship with the local community and, before long, children of some of the helpers were coming in after school and talking to both residents and helpers, and singing the songs they were taught at school, and telling them all about their day. It soon became apparent that this help which had been on a fairly casual basis was not enough, and it was decided to consider employing a resident member of staff, mainly to look after the dining room, serve meals and to get afternoon tea for the guests. Over a period they had several people but no one stayed for long, as many found Cropthorne too isolated from everyone and everything they knew. One or two who came were students who only wanted to fill in time between school and college. It was realised that what the house really needed was someone more permanent, who would stay for some time and would also be in sympathy with the work and aims of the house.

This problem was soon to be solved by a member of a group on retreat. Described in those days as a 'Moral Welfare Worker', she was in effect a social worker working with young unmarried mothers. She approached those running the *Old House*, and asked how they coped with the work and staffing the house. It appeared that, in her capacity as a social worker, she had a young woman with a small boy, whom she wished to place in a suitable live-in situation. This most fortuitous approach came just at the time when a more permanent, long-term assistant was being sought. Apparently the girl had begun her training at a Domestic Service College in London, but had been unable to finish the course due to the birth of her son. Her social worker felt that she would be reliable and well suited to the needs and aims of the *Old House*.

A committee was by now involved in the running of the house and after much consideration it was agreed that she should be asked to join the staff of the *Old House*. Peggy and her four-month-old son Stephen arrived, and were to stay for three happy years. Soon Peggy was taking over most of the cooking from Gladys Mayes, and helping with tasks that were becoming too much for her, with so many more people now visiting and resident at the house. Inevitably in those days there was criticism from some in the village who saw the employment of an unmarried mother as unacceptable. In her recollections Gladys remembered that the person who was at first most against Peggy's employment was so impressed by her willingness and ability to learn that she was the first to invite her to her home to meet her own daughters. She quickly became a very good friend to Peggy, accompanying her to the children's clinic, where she soon made friends amongst the other young mothers. Before very long she also became a member of the village's Women's Institute: a very positive result for a house concerned with caring and Christian values.

Some three years later, the *Old House* was host to a very happy event, the celebration of a wedding. A young family with whom Peggy had become very friendly moved away from the village and, after they had settled in their new home, asked Peggy if she could visit them for a short holiday. This she did and, on her return told everyone at Holland House and her friends in Cropthorne, that she had met a young man whilst on holiday and they had become good friends. He wanted to see her again, so she asked if it was possible for Frank to spend some part of his holiday in the village. It was arranged for him to stay in the home of one of the villagers, during the morning he helped the gardener with the digging and picking fruit or did various other odd jobs around the house as needed. The afternoons he spent with Peggy and her little boy, getting to know them even better.

Shortly after Frank returned home, a letter was received from his mother asking if Peggy could go and stay with her family for a few days. Frank very much wanted to marry Peggy, although he had apparently not yet proposed, and her future mother-in-law thought it would be an ideal opportunity to get to know her. Everyone agreed that this visit should be made and Peggy went to stay with Frank's family. On her return she told everyone that she and Frank were planning to get married in the following spring. The wedding took place in Cropthorne church, up the street from the *Old House*, with the management committee giving permission for the reception to be held in the house. Peggy's grandparents, Frank's parents and a number of friends travelled to Cropthorne for the marriage service, where they were joined by many friends from the village and of course everyone from the *Old House*. The wedding and the reception were very happy events and, although everyone was sad to lose Peggy and Stephen, they were so very pleased that the story should have a happy ending. It has been a long and happy marriage, of some 45 years at the time this history was written.

The next live-in helper stayed only a short time. She was followed by a charming Italian girl who spoke not a word of English when she arrived. Quick to learn sufficient basic phrases, she was very hard-working, and was soon able to look after the dining room. A Roman Catholic, she and another Italian girl also living in the village went to Sunday Mass at the Catholic Church in Pershore, but she would say her daily prayers in the quiet of the chapel in the *Old House*. Unfortunately she finally left, enticed away by her friend who was earning more money in a factory.

First Group Visits

As has already been mentioned, Bishop Cash was to make good use of the *Old House*, bringing groups of clergy to spend Monday to Friday in the peace of the house, garden and the chapel. That chapel is now the library and had previously been Mrs Holland's study. Later many of these visitors were to return with their wives to show them and to share with them the peace and beauty of it all. From these personal visits arose group visits from members of the Mothers Union, who came for a peaceful afternoon and tea. Later these short visits became residential weekends for members of Mothers Union groups throughout the Diocese and from many parishes.

The reputation and use of the *Old House* was growing rapidly and soon it became only too obvious that what items of bed linen and soft furnishings were available were beginning to wear out and replacements were still very difficult to obtain. Although a certain amount of army surplus had been obtained, more items were needed. A search was made through all the cupboards in the house, and this unearthed a quantity of curtains and some other material. The curtains were soon transformed into bedspreads and chair covers, the other material turned into cushion covers and other necessary items. 'Make do and mend' was a favourite slogan, even officially endorsed by the government in those days: certainly all the staff at the *Old House* fulfilled the injunction to their utmost.

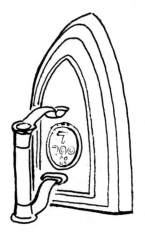

4

Expansion to Overflowing

So very popular was the Old House by now that it often happened that groups wanting to come were too big to be accommodated in the sixteen beds available. When possible, Mrs Holland allowed the use of one of her bedrooms. The Vicar, the Revd James Cathcart Davies (Vicar of Cropthorne 1936–55) and his wife also lent extra accommodation, although this was only available when their sons were away from home. The most memorable occasion on which a large group wanted to come was probably when a group of young people from Coventry wanted to make a booking. None of these spare rooms would be available, so the organizer was asked if it was possible to reduce the size of the party. He suggested that rather than do that, they should all bring camp beds and sleeping bags. This they did, filling their coach to overflowing. Their stay was for a week, and although at night every available space was occupied by camp beds, the visit was a great success and they visited on many more occasions.

The *Old House* was now becoming a favourite venue not only for clergy and Mothers Union events but for youth organisations throughout Worcester diocese. Every year the Anglican Young People's Association came, and the Worcester Youth Organiser arranged many visits of young people. Ken Weaver, who came to the Old House as a member of his youth club which was attached to St George's Church and affiliated

31

to AYPA, wrote 'Cropthorne is a wonderful place... the retreat house quiet and beautiful.' It is recalled by Gladys how very good these young people were, keen to help and do odd jobs: they would turn their hand to whatever needed doing, gardening, painting furniture and even decorating rooms.

Soon the Sunday-school organiser was to plan a visit which was to create what was probably the first 'tradition' at the *Old House*. Twice a year, a party of Sunday-school teachers arrived, one of these visits always being over the Whitsun bank-holiday weekend. It quickly became the 'tradition' to climb Bredon Hill on Whit Monday afternoon, those unable to walk all the way being transported part of the way by car, joining the others for the final trip to the summit. After such an expenditure of energy the whole party always came home ravenous to find that a good substantial tea had been prepared for their enjoyment. Those who came from town were particularly appreciative of the surrounding countryside and of course the lovely gardens belonging to the house.

The house was run on very happy and informal lines, young people would help with the odd job and decorating; washing-up was nearly always a communal effort. This all made for a great sense of community, which became one of the hallmarks of time spent at the *Old House*.

Brook House is Acquired

Those running the *Old House* realised that its reputation and success were creating a problem. Simply the house was not big enough. Providentially just at this time a house in the village, a little lower down the hill from the *Old House*, came on the market. *Brook House* was bought by Mrs Holland for the use of the retreat house to enlarge it facilities, particularly so that more overnight guests might be accommodated. Later, in 1954, the Diocese was to buy *Brook House* and in 1962 to sell it in order to finance the building of a new wing as it was felt that it was preferable to house all the facilities of the retreat house under one roof.

Appeals were issued throughout the Diocese for help in furnishing and equipping *Brook House*. The response was amazing, and soon everyone was busy sorting, cleaning and painting furniture, altering curtains and preparing the house for future guests: it was a tremendous task. The house itself required a great deal of cleaning, and much work needed to be carried out on the interior. A large roomy building, it had a drawing room on the ground floor big enough to hold quite major meetings or conferences as well as a number of bedrooms, which of course increased the overall capacity for parties.

A slightly new departure developed from the lack of group bookings for August. This holiday month was obviously not a good one for groups planning residential retreats or prayer weekends, so it was decided that the month should be given over to individual guests. Some of those who came had visited the *Old House* previously as a member of a group, others were coming for the first time. Gladys Mayes remembers some very charming visitors and, although not all were Anglicans, they all used the chapel for meditation and prayer. Everyone who came loved the gardens and the countryside and many of those who came singly were to return frequently. One particular visitor came regularly for retreats but always found her way into the kitchen for a while each morning. Here she would help with the washing-up, prepare fruit and vegetables for the meals and generally make herself useful in a very homely way. As Sybil put it, 'She became a very good friend to the House.'

From the very beginning, the gardens have always been one of the major attractions at the *Old House*. At first, Mrs Holland's gardener was able to manage the garden, and keep it looking really lovely, with just the help of a young boy. However, after a time Mrs Holland needed her gardener to undertake more work in her own gardens and it became necessary to employ a full-time gardener for the house. It was a great deal for one man to cope with on his own, and this is where very often staff and visitors would lend a hand. Apart from the lawns, flower beds, rose garden and walks, the gardens had many fruit trees and bushes. There were apples, plum and cherries as well as the less common mulberries. Where the car park now is, at the bottom of the garden overlooking the river were all manner of soft fruits, blackcurrants, redcurrants, raspberries, while figs grew in the kitchen garden. With food still very strictly rationed, all these home-grown fruits as well as the vegetables in the kitchen garden helped feed the visitors. Even when food became easier to obtain, the plentiful supplies of fruit and vegetables helped the staff to keep to the tight budget that was necessary to run the house successfully.

One summer during those early years, there was such a glut of apples, pears and plums that the branches of the trees could hardly support them, and were in great danger of breaking. With so much fruit everywhere, it was impossible to sell any, it could not even be given away, and there was too much to be used immediately for residents, guests and staff. However, a very good friend of the house lent them a canning machine belonging to the Women's Institute. As it was during the month of August when they had individual visitors rather than more formal retreats, the guests came to the rescue. On one occasion they managed to prepare and can 144 tins of fruit in one day. This wonderful harvest was a tremendous help during the winter months and after that glut year it became the practice to can and preserve fruit and vegetables every year.

In 1958 Mrs Holland celebrated her 80th birthday. The intention was to have a small private celebration on the Sunday. This would be after the sung Eucharist which was usually held in the church on the first Sunday of the month, and which Mrs Holland usually attended. Coffee was to be served and everyone was to have a piece of the birthday cake.

However, there was a group staying at the house who wanted
a quiet Sunday, so the party was changed to the Saturday
afternoon. Not only was the day changed, news of the celebration had leaked out into the village and, as Gladys Mayes
was to describe it later, '... various people arrived, bringing
flowers and presents until the dining room was quite
packed.' Mrs Holland was surprised and delighted, and cut
the cake while a photographer from the local paper took
several pictures. The staff members had asked Mrs Holland
what she would like for a birthday gift, and she asked for a
prayer book for the priest's stall in the parish church. This
was presented to her at the party and remained in the church
until replaced by the *Alternative Service Book*. This 'joining in'
by so many people in the village was very much their way of
life at that time. Gwendoline Blizard and Mamie both recall
how the *Old House* was so very much part of the whole village
in those days. The Deaconess and her sister are still spoken
of as showing so much kindness to everyone; there was
obviously a great warmth between the sisters and those living
in the village. Another link between house and village was
the local Choral Society whose members met and rehearsed
in the dining room at the *Old House*.

The beautiful rose-garden at the side of the house, near
the present chapel, came about due to the necessity of felling
a large elm tree growing at the side of the house very near
the road. In about 1959 the tree was deemed unsafe, and
could have fallen across the road, causing considerable dam-
age or injury. It was therefore necessary to fell the elm,
allowing it to fall within the garden across the yew hedge.
Everyone was sorry to see the tree go, as it was a great haunt
of birds, particularly of cuckoos who would sit calling in the
tree every spring. They were said to be particularly noisy
during services in the chapel since the tree was adjacent to
the window. After the tree was felled, the garden looked
rather a mess: the hedge was slightly damaged and the area

around the remains of the tree was left untidy with no particular plan or design.

As it happened, the brother of Deaconess and Gladys Mayes visited them for a weekend at about that time. Asked what he thought should be done with the area of what Sybil called 'miserable' garden, he suggested that it would make an ideal rose garden. This seemed an excellent idea, and it was decided to approach friends and those who used the house frequently, if they would like to give a rose bush or make a donation towards one. Soon there was the beginning of a fine rose-garden and later more trees were added to create what was to become a favourite place for visitors who wanted a quiet, peaceful place for meditation.

Forming 'the Friends'

This informal giving by friends was a precursor of a more formal way of creating friends and helping the *Old House*. It was becoming obvious that items of furnishings, carpets and equipment were beginning to need replacement. Most importantly of all, the house was in need of re-thatching. Although there were many friends who gave generously in the form of gifts to the house, there was no formal group of 'Friends of the Retreat House'. It was suggested that such a group could be formed, of people willing to promise an annual donation or subscription to the house, thus giving a possibly small but regular income. The idea was welcomed and in 1960 was put into practice. To set up such an organisation required a considerable amount of work and planning. In the first place, the committee contacted the leaders of all the groups who had visited the house, along with others who had visited as individuals. They were invited to a service of thanksgiving for the work of the house, the service to be followed by a lunch. The response to this invitation was wonderful, well over a hundred people promising to come.

Mrs Ellis Holland.

'The Den' with barn and pump, early 1900's.

Sketch from a photograph taken in 1909.

New Gable, Sunken Garden and Sundial.

Dovecote and view over the river.

Mayday celebration, probably 1928.
(reproduced by kind permission of Mrs Ida Baker.)

'The Old House' *c.* 1928.
(reproduced by kind permission of Mrs Ida Baker.)

Presentation to the Vicar *c.* 1954. Mrs Holland (2nd left), Olaf
Bloomfield (3rd) and The Revd and Mrs Cathcart-Davies.
(reproduced by kind permission of Mrs Ida Baker.)

Deaconess Mayes (3rd left).

St Michael's Church, McCreary, Manitoba, Canada. Mrs Holland instigated much fund raising for the building of this church.

Clergy course on administration. Front row right, Miss Munro, Miss James and the Revd Julian Dawes.

The Chapel, 1960.

The Library, c. 1976

The Chapel.

Building the Conference Room.

The Conference Room and bedrooms.

The Conference Room. Pupils from Ellerslie School.

The Dining Room. Old fireplace with Delft tiles.

An aerial view of Holland House.

Holland House today.

Painting Course, 1993. Ted Newman and Sylvia Pierce.

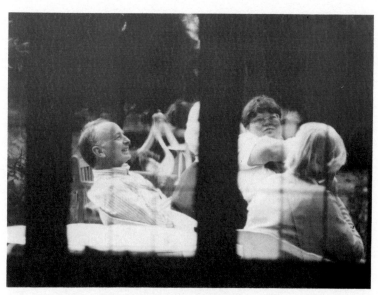

Through the dining room window – Martley Parish
Conference, 1994.

At the dedication of the Chapel, September 1965, Miss Evelyn
James with the Dean of Worcester, Bishop of Worcester and
Archdeacon of Worcester.

William Swabey and Peter Middlemiss, 1994.

Peter Middlemiss and fellow members of the executive,
Ecumenical Association of Academies and Laity Centres in
Europe after an audience with the Romanian Patriarch, 1995.

On a glorious summer day, a service of thanksgiving was conducted in the parish church by the vicar, the Reverend Peter Wylie. (Vicar of Cropthorne 1958–61) The church was packed, and those who have spoken or written of it since have all said that it was a very beautiful service; the Bishop of Worcester was also present on that most memorable day. After lunch had been served at Brook House and people had taken the opportunity to walk in the gardens, the Bishop gave a talk in the garden of the Old House. After tea, the guests began to leave for home and thus ended the inaugural meeting of the 'Friends of the Old House'. It was declared a great success by the committee and staff, and well worth while all the effort.

Although this first meeting of the 'Friends' was a great success there was not to be another such meeting the following year. Changes and developments were taking place, plans were being made to enlarge the house to increase the number of people able to be resident. Although Brook House was large and could accommodate a number of people, it was not always easy for residents to turn out late at night to walk down the hill, especially in the winter. It was also expensive to heat, sometimes only for a few people.

The other major change was the departure of the two sisters who had been such an important part of the early days of the Old House. At the beginning of 1961, Deaconess Sybil Mayes had a period of illness and was advised to take a long rest. After consulting with the Bishop, she decided that it would be best to give up her position as Warden at the Old House, and in June of that year she and her sister left with many regrets, but in the knowledge that they had contributed greatly to the success of the retreat house. It had been hard work but as Gladys was to say many years later, 'We had a time of real enjoyment and made so many good friends.' On leaving the Old House, Deaconess Mayes and her sister went to the vicarage at Crowle. Gladys is now (1995) living in

Worcester, her sister having died only a fairly short time before.

New Warden and More Developments

A new warden had now to be appointed. By a fortunate coincidence for Cropthorne, *St Anne's*, the Gloucester Diocesan House at Cheltenham, was being closed temporarily and the Warden and her colleague would have to be made redundant. Deaconess Mayes was aware of the situation at Cheltenham, and mentioned it to the Bishop of Worcester, the Rt Revd Charles Edwards. The Bishop and his wife went to Cheltenham to meet both Evelyn James the Warden at *St Anne's*, and Kay Munro her colleague, to ask whether they would consider undertaking similar work at Cropthorne. The outcome of this visit was that Evelyn James agreed to come to the *Old House* as Warden and Kay Munro accompanied her as the Housekeeper. They took up their new duties at the *Old House* in the summer of 1961.

The newcomers had been at Cropthorne for ten months when the work began on the major restructuring and building which was necessary to turn the *Old House* into an efficient and viable retreat house. It was necessary to close the house for some time to allow the work to go ahead, as the first phase was to modernise the existing accommodation before building a new wing.

In the autumn of 1962, work began on re-plumbing the house to give fitted washbasins in all the rooms, at the same time three new bathrooms were added. Plenty of constant hot water for personal and domestic use was ensured by the provision of two large boilers, which also provided central heating throughout. What a change from the old days!

By this time, the house had a properly constituted Management Committee, the Chairman being the Ven. Peter Eliot, Archdeacon of Worcester. There was also a Committee of Friends which has been chaired by, among others: the Ven.

Peter Eliot; Stanley Packman; the Revd David Rhodes, Vicar of Astwood Bank; Richard Mumford; and the Revd J.P. Lankester, Vicar of Stockton-on-Teme. The Diocese was giving some considerable financial support to the house, which was officially described as a Diocesan Retreat House. With this support and backing from the 'Friends', it was felt possible to continue the second part of the development, the new wing.

The building of this new block was interrupted by another exceptionally hard winter. Immediately after the Christmas of 1962 the whole country awoke to find a deep covering of snow. This snow was to remain in much of the country for up to three months, with the earth frozen to a depth of several feet. Even very deep water mains froze solid, and most building work ceased for many weeks. Foundations could not be dug in the frozen ground and bricklaying, concreting and roofing were all impossible. Evelyn James tells how, immediately after the Christmas holiday ended, the workmen came to collect their tools and did not return until March. They then had to thaw out the piles of bricks with blow lamps.

Brook House was sold in January, causing another practical problem in that freezing weather. The entire contents of the house had to be transported up the hill to the *Old House* for storage. The roads almost impassable with rutted frozen snow, ice and drifts. The task was finally accomplished and the entire contents of *Brook House* were removed, most ending up stacked in the dining room at the *Old House*, which Evelyn James described as looking like a 'Pickford's Repository' (warehouse).

When building work was finally recommenced, it was still bitterly cold, and every day Kay made a large and very welcome lunchtime pan of soup for the dozen or so men working on the site. Then, just as spring arrived and it seemed that work could go ahead at full speed, another happier event called a halt to some of the building. One morning in May one of the workmen came to the back-door and, looking rather worried and very apologetic, explained that work on one part of the new wing would have to wait. There were groans all round at this further delay — what now? He explained that a blackbird was sitting on her nest in one of the half-built bedrooms in the new wing. It was agreed that she could not possibly be disturbed and must remain until the young had hatched and flown.

However, despite the appalling weather at the beginning of the year, as well as the need to provide maternity accommodation for blackbirds, the work continued. At the beginning of October 1963, with the varnish hardly dried on the new bannisters, all was completed and ready for the first bookings. The new wing contained sixteen bedrooms on two floors, and a fine conference room on the ground floor. The house was now able to accommodate 28 people in 20 single rooms and four twin-bedded rooms. No longer were there problems with the water supply and the one bathroom, each room now had a wash-basin with hot and cold running water, and there were also now seven bathrooms. Oil-fired central heating had been installed throughout. A later brochure advertising the house in January 1971 stresses that bed linen, soap and towels are provided and that there is a plentiful supply of hot water. Things had come a long way since the 1940s.

Funding for this major project had come partly from the sale of *Brook House* by the Diocese, partly from an anonymous gift of £5,000, the sale of some of the orchard and a legacy from the 'Cutler Bequest'. The Revd Canon C.E. Cutler, who died on 15th July 1959, devised his house *Rosehill* in Worcester to the Diocesan Bishop to be used as 'the latter might direct'. The property was sold for £15,800, and the greater part of these proceeds was devoted to the renovations and rebuilding at the *Old House*.

The sixteen new bedrooms were furnished by the deaneries and Cathedral Chapter of the Diocese. These rooms have plaques attached to their doors identifying by whom they were 'adopted' A reception and service to celebrate the re-opening of the Diocesan Retreat and Conference Centre were held on 31st October 1963. After a reception for the guests at 2.30 p.m., there was then tea, followed by Evensong in the parish church of Cropthorne, the address being given by the Bishop of Worcester.

In the following year the purpose-built chapel was designed and built. Both these major building projects were designed by Maurice W. Jones ARIBA, the Diocesan Architect, together with his associate B. Wallis De Russet, ARIBA. The builders were Messrs W.A. Cox of Evesham, whose Chairman Major T.L. Cox presented the altar rails for the new chapel in memory of his father W.A. Cox, who had died three years earlier. The floor tiles in the chapel were made by the Malvern Tile Company. Naturally all the building work, particularly that around the site for the chapel did no good at all to the beautiful gardens. However, the gardener Bronislaus Leisaunieks followed hard on the heels of the builders, and adapted the deigns so that soon they were back to their original beauty.

The minutes of a meeting held on 28th February 1964 detail the discussion regarding the furnishing and decor for the new chapel. Those present consisted of the Archdeacon of Worcester, the Revd Dr Peter Moore of Pershore Abbey, Miss Evelyn James the Warden, and the architects Maurice W. Jones and B.W. De Rusett. Simplicity and clean lines were to be the guidelines. There would be a simple stone altar, placed so that the celebrant could officiate from either side; the sanctuary to be on one level. The solid free-standing stone altar that was placed in the chapel on its completion was the gift of Mrs Grosvenor, widow of the Revd J.E. Grosvenor, who had until a short time before his death been Chairman of the Old House Committee. The matching paving for the sanctuary was given by his family.

Both the altar and the paving were the work of Ben Davis of Worcester.

There was to be no cross or rood, nor any cross on the altar, just low candlesticks to the architects' design. It was felt that the framework of the window was in itself an expression of the cross, and maybe at a later date simple designs could be etched into the clear glass. Rather than traditional pews, a preference for chairs was agreed and, instead of a credence table, it was decided that a simple shelf should be built into the side wall, possibly using slate.

The service of dedication of the newly completed chapel was held on 12th September 1964, at 3 p.m. Among those present were the Archdeacons of Worcester, the Dean of Worcester, the Assistant Bishop, the Bishop's Chaplain and the Lord Bishop. The act of dedication was performed by the Rt Revd L.M. Charles Edwards, Bishop of Worcester, who also gave the address. Also taking part in the procession were the Master Builder W.A Cox, and the Warden Miss Evelyn James. There is at Holland House a very fine book produced to celebrate the completion and dedication of the new chapel. As well as giving a brief, and regrettably rather inaccurate, history of the house, it also lists all the gifts and donations made by the 'Friends' since their formation in 1961, as well as many gifts from individuals. Among the gifts from other churches and parishes is the very practical gift of a 'large double boiler, baking trays and tins' from the Parish of Christ-church and All Saints, Cockermouth, in the Diocese of Carlisle — a very far-flung group of 'Friends' indeed. The fine calligraphy of this book is on hand-made paper. The book cost £100 to produce and was considered by some at that time to have been an unnecessary expense, but many years later it can be seen as a memento of a very happy occasion.

The 'Friends' were by now a most vital aspect of the running and financing of the house. They contributed to the garden and its running expenses as well as to the those of the Old House itself and much of its necessary equipment.

In the early days of the retreat house there was no official car park, but this was fast becoming an absolute necessity. Under the chairmanship of Richard Mumford, the House applied for planning permission, and a car park was constructed on the area of land now occupied by the bungalow known as *The Den*. This was fairly small and would not suffice for long. As parking restrictions became ever tighter, and more and more people wanted to arrive singly by car, it became necessary to create a much larger parking area. In about 1982 a large area at the bottom of the garden, overlooking the river, was landscaped and a car park constructed. This was an ideal place for a car park as, given the slope of the gardens, it is invisible from the house as well as from the major portion of the grounds.

Fourteen Years of Activity

During the next fourteen years, the work of the Diocesan Retreat House at Cropthorne was to grow and develop. Adding to the retreats and conferences that had already been part of the life of the house, there was now an increased interest from outside the Diocese as well as a great deal of interest from the clergy and the many organisations belonging to the Worcester Diocese.

Bishop Robin Woods instituted clergy schools, and about fifteen of these took place over a period of three years, with about twenty members of the clergy attending each one. These clergy retreats lasted just under a full week, and at each one a particular aspect of ministry was studied. There were also ordination retreats, conducted retreats and training days. A number of parish groups came for short weekend retreats, sometimes rather apprehensive as to what a retreat would be like, but it was apparent from the response and follow-up that all found the experience rewarding, and asked to come again.

Among the many young people who visited the Old House was a very appreciative group from a residential home for the mentally handicapped in Bromsgrove. The twelve youngsters and their care staff all felt that they had gained a great deal from the visit.

Another series of 'Quiet Days' was held for boys from King's School, Worcester, and girls from four of the boarding schools in Malvern, prior to their Confirmation. Brought by their respective Chaplains, it is recalled by one of these Chaplains that in every case 'their quest for spiritual sustenance was equalled by their appetites and their appreciation of the meals was enough to delight the heart of any cook'. When the school-leaving age was raised to sixteen, there were parties of school leavers who came for three days in their last term. These three days were spent in a variety of occupations, community service in a home for the elderly, or in a day nursery, pony-riding, canoeing, and orienteering on the Malvern Hills. Weather permitting, some of these groups were able to have supper parties on the river bank at the bottom of the garden, cooking sausages over a camp fire, and rowing on the river in the calm of the evening.

The Chapel has twice been the venue for weddings, on each occasion the bride was the daughter of a member of the Diocesan clergy. One of the brides was the daughter of the vicar Julian Dawes and his Danish wife Dorte. Lone Grove (née Dawes) recalls with especial pleasure her wedding in May 1972, the Nuptial Mass in the Chapel, with the reception in the house, 'It was very special to be able to use the chapel and beautiful grounds.' For each wedding, the celebration of the Nuptial Mass in the Chapel was followed by a reception in the oak-beamed dining room, and there is no doubt that the beautiful *Old House* and its gardens would have created a wonderful atmosphere and setting for such a happy and important occasion. A further highlight for the House and Chapel was a visit from the Archbishop of Canterbury, Dr Michael Ramsey. The Archbishop was visiting Evesham at the time, and was brought over to Cropthorne by the Bishop. In the Visitor's book, his signature, Michael Cantuar, was followed by his entry in which he wrote:

Today I visited this lovely Retreat House.

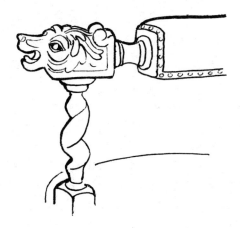

5

'From Diocesan Retreat House to A Christian Centre for Individual and Group Renewal'

Although the *Old House* was extremely successful as a place of spiritual retreat, the financial aspect was not so good. Unfortunately there was no significant use of the house from Monday to Friday, apart from the mid-week clergy schools. In 1974 there were fewer of these schools than there had been in the previous two years, and it was becoming obvious that serious thought would have to be given to the future if the Retreat House was to survive.

In 1974 a Bishop's Working Party was convened to discuss the future of the House. This working party's remit was to discuss whether the work could continue and, if so, what form it should take and how it should be financed. Among the many difficulties and problems revealed in the report of the working party were, principally, high cost of maintenance of house and grounds, possible understaffing, a poorly-equipped kitchen and the purchasing of food in small quantities with poor portion control. Rapidly rising inflation at that period meant that the individual had less money to spend and naturally a residential retreat had to come fairly low on most people's list of priorities. To quote from the standing committee's report:

> ... it is the experience of this Diocese, as elsewhere, that there is a general lack of recruits for residential conferences, where people have to pay for themselves, and attend in their own time. At Cropthorne the majority of the 'market' falls into this category....
>
> The usual reaction to increased costs is for the vendor to raise his prices. Business sense seems to dictate that this should happen at Cropthorne, but we are persuaded that there comes a time of counter-productivity when the consequent cancellations or lack of bookings, outweigh the increased revenue from higher prices.

The report also commented on one very serious financial drawback. There were no endowment funds available to the *Old House*: it was noted that a similar retreat house (unfortunately no longer in existence as a retreat house) in the Birmingham Diocese had received significant sums of money each year as a result of bequests and investments.

Obviously, certain very serious questions had to be discussed. The working party was therefore asked to consider three main points.

a) Is there a need for a Diocesan House?
b) If so, of what kind should it be?
c) Can we afford to provide and run such an establishment?

At this stage the working party was interpreting '... Diocesan House to mean a residential establishment, and have disregarded matters that would concern day use only.' A number of courses of action were considered. These included: 'simultaneous conferences, short courses run successively during a weekend i.e. Friday/Saturday, Saturday/Sunday, and also using vacant rooms for individuals who wished to come for quiet and prayer'.

It was accepted that these changes, whilst they would not increase costs greatly, would also not add much to the income and would certainly not be far-reaching enough to solve the problems of the house.

It was thought possible to realise some assets, as had been done when the new wing was built. To this end, a list of possible assets was drawn up. These included selling *Vine Cottage* (the gardener's cottage) selling land for building, and even leasing the river frontage for leisure purposes. For various reasons, including difficulty in obtaining planning permission, loss of access and amenities, especially to the river, and the time all this would take, ruled out most realisation of assets. Finally it was decided that there were seven courses of action open, namely:

1. status quo, with minor adjustments;
2. realisation of some assets;
3. partnership with another body;
4. reorganisation with a warden/trainer;
5. realisation of all assets, and provision elsewhere;
6. regional co-operation;
7. winding up.

It was agreed that suggestions 1, 5 and 6 were unlikely to solve the problem and that winding up the house would be an unacceptable answer in so far as the Diocese was concerned, except in the direst circumstance.

The final decision had to be made by the Diocesan Synod, the working party could only make recommendations. There were difficult decisions to be taken, not least because they involved individuals as well as matters purely financial.

The final paragraph of the report of the working party stressed this need to take regard of the loyalty and hard work of all those who had been involved with the *Old House* over so many years.

> Those who have conducted the affairs of the *Old House*, in management, as staff and as Friends, have done so with a dedication and willingness that has greatly impressed us. We wish unreservedly to pay tribute to their efforts in providing the service they have under very difficult conditions for so

long.... We wish to ask that the utmost care should be taken
to see that all concerned, and especially Miss James, Miss
Munro and the gardener, are treated fairly and sensitively in
whatever decisions are made.

Searching for an Answer Through Prayer

There were at the same time other thoughts and ideas put
forward by members of the 'Friends' of the *Old House* as to
what it could be best used for. On the night of Friday 6th
December 1974 it was decided, at Miss Munro's suggestion,
that a 'Pray-in' should be held at the *Old House*. During the
night a continuous twelve-hour vigil was kept, and over 60
people attended during those hours. The next morning over
40 people were present at the 8 o'clock communion service.
In addition there were many who wrote regretting that they
could not be present but saying that they would be praying
for the house and giving their full support to whatever was
decided for the future.

On 12th December, the then chairman of the 'Friends',
Richard Mumford, wrote to members listing some of the
ideas that had been put forward, and detailing the small
working party that had been set up to consider these ideas.
The working party was to consist of the Secretary, the Chaplain and himself.

The many ideas for the use of the house included the
running of the house by a community, and its use for: '... holiday,
art, drama and very strongly it came out that people had in
mind a healing centre, a place of refreshment'.
After the first meeting of the working party, four considera-
tions were put forward for discussion. It was agreed that until
the end of February 1975 all 'Friends' would pray for the *Old
House* daily at eight o'clock every morning. Richard Mumford
suggested that the headings as listed would be excellent
ideas and thoughts on which to concentrate one's prayers.
1.   The *Old House* should be taken by Trustees (who should
     these be?) at a nominal rent from the diocese and the

Trustees would be responsible for running the house, not the diocese. The diocese would, of course, have the opportunity of booking the house when it is available for conferences, etc.

2. The use of the house could be, in some form, a place for married, pre-marriage and post-marriage couples, particularly those with marriage problems, where they could come for guidance, rest, refreshment and of course with their family.
3. Source of income, who would pay for these couples?
4. Staffing. What staff is required: Warden? Cook? community, and where would these people live?

6

New Plans
and a New Direction

At the Diocesan Synod in March 1975, the report of these discussions was presented, and the officers of the Friends were instructed to implement the report with a view to 'finding an economic use within the present structure'. During the next Diocesan Synod on 9th July 1975, Richard Mumford, as chairman of the Friends, was allowed to put forward the final proposal. Previously the occupancy of the house had been only 20%, costing the diocese £4000 – £5000 per year. The Friends were aiming at 35% occupancy, at which point they felt they would break even. It was suggested:

> ... that they would form an independent trust and run the house commercially, providing perhaps a refuge for ex-prisoners, battered wives, etc.

It was appreciated that there would be some concern among local residents, including Lady Goodbody, a niece of Mrs Holland, as to the effect such an establishment would have on village life, especially as the house was so centrally placed in Cropthorne. Before Synod could give its approval to the plans put forward by the Friends, it was clear that any trust to be set up was necessarily subject to the approval of the Diocesan Trustees and the Diocesan Board of Finance. Bishop Robin Woods and the Archdeacon, the Venerable

Peter Eliot, were totally behind the proposal to set up an independent trust. However, although the plans for a trust went ahead, the thoughts of using the house as a refuge were dropped.

It was at this point that a group from Coventry came on the scene; most importantly Miss Diana Day, who was to play a major part in the future of what would soon become Holland House. Diana was a teacher of classics and drama, first of all in her home county of Sussex and then Kent where she had responsibility for Classics, Drama and sixth-form studies. In January of 1959 she arrived in the City of Coventry to take up a senior post in a large comprehensive school. Diana had felt for some time prior to taking up this appointment that it was inevitable that she would find herself in Coventry, as she once wrote, '... it was the Cathedral that seemed to be calling me.'

Certainly something seemed to be calling Diana to a different way of life, and she soon realised that she wanted a life other than that of a senior post in a large school. Over a period of months several ideas were considered. Together with friends who, like her, sought a more spiritual dimension to their lives, they considered forms of communal and/or Christian artistic life. Diana sold her house as her share towards a possible venture into community life, but the great problem was finding a suitable property. After several false starts, Diana was told by the Ven. Peter Eliot that the Diocese of Worcester was considering selling the *Old House*, as they could no longer afford its running costs. The house was already known to her, as she had visited on a previous occasion. The Friends of the House were trying hard to prevent the sale, and initial contact with Diana Day started a series of meetings, both in Coventry and Cropthorne. Together with Diana were John and Maxine Cook and a young postgraduate student, Kathryn Spink, who wanted to give her postgraduate year to this work. Kate's Father was a Canon of Coventry Cathedral, John Cook was Head Verger

at the Cathedral, and Maxine his wife had catering experience.

A party of the Friends travelled to Coventry where Maxine
cooked a wonderful meal and there was much discussion as
to the future. Diana was very conscious that they would be
working to a very tight budget. Worcester Diocese as a whole
was encouraging but they all realised that the project would
be impossible without the help of the Friends: Archdeacon
Peter Eliot in particular was a great supporter of their hopes
and plans, as was the Bishop of Worcester, Robin Woods and
his wife Mrs Henrietta Woods. The idea was gradually for-
mulated that the 'Friends' should take over the running of
the house as an independent trust. The Trustees were to be
appointed from amongst the members of the Friends.

The final agreement was that the four should run the
house for the first year, each of them taking £1,000 as a small
stipend. The diocese was prepared to let the *Old House* at a
peppercorn rent for one year: there was, however, a proviso.
The diocese required the 'Friends' to show money or guarantees of not less than £10,000 in order that, should the
project fail (as apparently many thought it would), the diocese would not be left with a debt; also, the house was to be
taken on a full repairing lease. Within a month, cash to the
value of £2,500 was raised and the necessary guarantees
assured; in fact more than the required sums were guaran-
teed, since pledges to a total of £20,000 were made.

The Trust took over the House on 17th January 1976,
Bishop Allenby serving as chairman of the trustees for the
first three years. In future the *Old House* would be known as
Holland House as a tribute and memorial to Mrs Holland.
Maxine was installed as Catering Manager, her husband John
was to be Caretaker and Gardener (with Bronislaw Leisaunieks — known to everyone as Bruno — remaining part-
time to train John). Diana was Warden and Director of
Studies. She lived in the main house, the Cooks and their

two children in a flat over the kitchen, and Kate had a room at the top of the house.

When the time came for the Trust to take over full responsibility for the running and maintenance of Holland House, the Vicar of Cropthorne, the Revd Julian Dawes, and his wife decided that, although they wished the new project every success, they did not see it as their particular métier, and therefore did not wish to become too deeply involved. This led to the appointment of the Revd Nicholas Brown to the living of Cropthorne, with the specific aim that he would work closely with the new team. Although it had been agreed originally that there would be no formal chaplaincy to Holland House, he was later accepted as their chaplain. All these changes necessarily meant that Evelyn James would retire as Warden, which was a sad time for her. To quote Richard Mumford:

> She moved out the day the new team moved in, and whilst she fully supported the project, was obviously sad at leaving, but at least the house was going forward.

Evelyn moved to Salisbury, and Kay went to live with her sister in Shrewsbury.

7
A Change of Style

There were to be a good many changes in the way of life at Holland House. In the style of retreat houses of that earlier period, the old regime had been rather austere in certain respects, notices abounded in all the rooms forbidding smoking, towels on bedspreads and slamming of doors as well as instructions as to where one should be quiet. Diana tells the story of the first time that she visited the *Old House* (with at that time no thought of ever running it). She and her fellow group members were required to be in by 9.30 p.m., or ask for a key and give their reasons for being out so late. As grown women holding senior posts, they were disinclined to have to give such explanations, so brought into use the outside fire escapes.

These notices disappeared and only minimal rules were kept to ensure the smooth running of the house, thus giving a more relaxed atmosphere when Diana and her team took over. Another immediately noticeable change was the removal of a rather brooding life-size statue of St Anne, which had been standing half-way up the main staircase.

Knowing how Diana felt about this figure, Kate, who had arrived the day before Diana, had arranged for it to be placed in her room to await her arrival! In researching the origins of the statue, it was discovered that it had come from the old St Anne's retreat house in Cheltenham. Furthermore it was

learned that it had originally been presented to the Cheltenham house by the sisters at Wantage. To quote Diana:

> A 'phone call to the sisters made it quite clear that they did
> not relish its return. They recommended a quiet, dignified
> disposal but warned us not to attempt drowning — they had
> themselves tried unsuccessfully to dispose of a statue by that
> method (an air pocket had remained within, and head and
> shoulders bobbed disconcertingly up and down in the water;
> retrieving the 'corpse' proved difficult!).

Finally a message to a master stonemason solved the problem, and the statue of St Anne was later seen in the show-
room of John Hopkins of Tewkesbury; there is no record of
her final resting place.

With the minor problem of the statue out of the way, there
came more major purges for the new team. The first was the
necessity for disposing of vast quantities of dried vegetables
that had been acquired and not used over several years. The
new team were fortunate in that there had recently been a
great deal of snow followed by prolonged heavy rainfall; this
had caused the infill from an unsuspected well to collapse,
the perfect burial place. With some ceremony the rather
ancient dried vegetables were interred and covered with
barrow-loads of soil. Occasional nightmare thoughts of more
rain reconstituting the vegetables and creating a swelling
amorphous mass, ready to engulf the house, proved un-
founded; they remained safely buried.

Also in the store cupboards were colossal tins of stewed
steak which did not really fit in with what was hoped to be
the new catering aspirations, but it was good food and could
not be wasted, what should be done? Fortunately Kate had
plenty of experience and great expertise in making curries,
having spent much of her life in India. So a new dish was
born, the tins reminded the team of dog food so 'Bengal
Bounce' arrived on the menu and was much appreciated by
everyone.

Following the problems of 'inherited stores' came the general difficulties of providing good wholesome food on a limited budget. Bruno and John kept Maxine well supplied with fresh vegetables, and there was soft fruit in season. Diana created a herb garden and there were also two greenhouses which were productive although, after a year or two, one collapsed from old age, assisted by a storm.

Diana and Maxine were in particular determined that vegetarian guests should not be presented with the inevitable boiled egg, alternating with an omelette, served with whatever vegetables were available with the main menu. As Diana already had some experience preparing vegetarian meals, she agreed with Maxine that she would 'mastermind' the vegetarian menus. Soon word spread that the 'veggie' menus at Holland House were something special, with plenty of beautifully cooked and presented home-grown fruit and vegetables to accompany excellent main-course dishes.

Vegans, who will eat no animal or dairy products at all, can create quite a problem when it comes to providing an interesting menu. The very first vegans that Diana had to provide for came with no warning at all, what should they do? With little time to plan, Diana rushed into the garden and, taking a handful of foliage from every plant that she knew to be edible, adding weeds such as young dandelion and fat hen, and a few flowers including borage, filled a large salad bowl. The result was delighted guests and Diana knew what to do in the future.

Home-made yogurt appeared on the menu when John decided that it would be good to keep a goat; a Togenburg was chosen and named Gambol, although she also had a very superior name by which she was known in the breed society. Gambol was accommodated in a commodious apartment in the stable next to Vine Cottage, where John and Maxine now lived. Some time later Gambol gave birth to twin kids, unfortunately both were male. Regrettably it was becoming apparent that, delightful though she was, the time and attention she needed could not really be justified, and it was decided that goat-keeping at Holland House should come to an end. Let it be said that this decision had nothing to do with the fact that Gambol had wrecked Diana's precious herb garden! This had occurred quite early on in Gambol's time at Holland House.

With a working capital of only £2,000 and only a few bookings, the new team had a daunting task before them. By July 1976 Bruno had moved out of *Vine Cottage* and the first necessity was to renew the electrical wiring. The quote for this was between £100 and £120, plus materials. There was really insufficient money, so the Revd John Dale, a very active and supportive member of the Friends, helped with the work, and it was completed by the team themselves.

During those early days, many unusual bookings were taken in order to provide the necessary income, Transcendental Meditation being one of the more unusual. However, the ideas that had been earlier entertained of having battered wives and ex-prisoners had been dropped as being rather too difficult to finance, and likely to produce only an uncertain income. It was proposed therefore to run the house as a 'Christian haven of rehabilitation, for those requiring rest and resuscitation'. Gradually this aim would crystallise into creating a haven for retreats and conferences.

The first truly massive expense faced by the Trustees was the re-thatching of the major part of the roof. The thatch had been partly repaired only two years before, but this had been inadequate; the work now needing to be done was likely to cost between £7,000 and £8,000. Fortunately a grant towards this cost was available, but there would be a wait of a year before the grant could be paid. In the meantime, other fund-raising events were organised, including dances — with a marquee on the tennis lawn, open days and garden days, all these well supported by the Friends and their friends.

Over the next few years much work was completed on the property, apart, that is, from the continual decorating and re-decorating of the exterior and the most-used public rooms. The kitchen was improved and modernised, Vine Cottage (now the home of the Warden) was extended, and the garages at the side of the house were converted into a two-bedroom bungalow and named *The Den* after the original house (this bungalow is now the home of the Deputy Warden). The much-needed car park was also created, and a large stone-paved area at the back by the main entrance. With new regulations coming into force regarding fire escapes, new external stairs had to be provided. Altogether in the last twenty years something in the region of £200,000 has been spent on maintenance and improvements. With all this practical work continuing around them, the team were very busy creating a place that would become well known for the breadth of its Christian commitment.

'Ecumenism at its Best'

To quote a Catholic priest, Father Terry Sheridan SCJ, who visited Holland House on two occasions: 'We found, and I re-discovered, ecumenism at its best.' Father Sheridan had visited Holland House in the late 1970s when he took two young men with him to a pre-noviciate retreat. One of the young men persevered and was ordained to the priesthood. Father Sheridan remembers the peace and beauty of the house and the wonderful hospitality they received. Particularly remaining in his mind '... was the privilege of being able to celebrate Mass in the chapel'. Father Sheridan returned to Holland House briefly in this jubilee year. He had also been in contact with the priest that he had brought with him on his first visit, who was all for organising another retreat in the near future. A sure sign, says Father Sheridan, '... that he too had been marked by his experience'.

This sense of ecumenical love and friendship is something that permeates the whole atmosphere of Holland House. Over recent years such a broad spectrum of events has developed that all who attend a retreat or conference or even visit for a brief meeting feel that there in Holland House is something special for them as individuals, no matter their particular denomination.

Diana Day and her team worked hard to create this very special environment for their work, and there is no doubt that they were successful. They sought to create what she has described as an 'interdenominational house where renewal, reconciliation and wholeness of life were paramount'. In this task there is absolutely no doubt that they succeeded. It was to be the misfortune of the House that, in the course of her work as Warden and Director of Studies, she should meet the former rector of the nearby village of Bredon, Canon Colin Beswick. They worked together as friends and colleagues for a long time but at the end of July in 1979 Diana left Holland House and she and Colin were married in the September. At the time of their marriage Colin was Director of Ministry for the Worcester Diocese.

During Diana's time at Holland House they were introduced to the Revd Jonathan Crane, previously a Minor Canon at St. George's Chapel Windsor: he first came partly as a guest and partly as a helper. His wife Meg was described by Richard Mumford as 'a delightful girl and a great support'. Jonathan helped Diana to a considerable degree, both with the booking and planning of courses. Apart from this practical aspect of his work, guests soon discovered in him a valued source of spiritual healing and counselling. When Diana left, Jonathan Crane took over the running of Holland House, continuing to work with John and Maxine Cook, Kathryn having left by then as her intended time at Holland House was only to be her postgraduate year. After Kathryn had left, Keith Davies joined the team full-time, he was extremely practical and of great help in the running of the house. To quote a member of the 'Friends' it would seem that, '... the regime with Jonathan Crane was a bit of a roller-coaster'. Times with Jonathan could be hectic and exciting, but some of the peaceful atmosphere of the house was lost, and eventually Jonathan left to become Priest-in-Charge at Harvington. There is no doubt that when Peter Middlemiss took over, he inherited from Jonathan a well staffed and organised house, everything was in very good order.

After Jonathan left and during the interim before Peter's arrival, Herbert Gawne-Caine and his wife stepped into the breach. The Gawne-Caines lived in an adjoining cottage to Holland House and had been of great help in the past, particularly with the book-keeping.

Apart from the success of the house as an ecumenical centre of excellence, another great practical achievement was that between 1976 and 1995 there was only one year when a loss was made. To quote Richard Mumford:

> It is a measure of the good management and use of the house and the support of the Friends, that it now shows a healthy balance sheet in spite of the large expenditure of capital over these twenty years.

Consolidation of Ecumenism

The next few years, bringing us up to the time of the golden jubilee, were indeed a consolidating of all the plans and hopes of those earlier days.

Peter Middlemiss was appointed as the new Warden in December 1983, He and his wife Fritha came from Derby-shire, where they had run Morley Rectory, a similar but slightly smaller retreat house some miles from Derby. Shortly after they arrived, Fritha began training for the Diaconate and was later among the first of the women deacons to be ordained a priest at Worcester Cathedral in 1994. As well as her parish work, Fritha is now one of the chaplains at Holland House, together with Kenneth Boyce the local vicar of Flad-bury, Cropthorne no longer having a resident incumbent.

On a purely practical level, one of the very first changes that Peter was to bring about at Holland House was the building of the new entrance from the gardens. This widened what had been passages from the hall and dining room to the drawing room into a wide reception hall, where tea and coffee are served between sessions, and where there is also a small bar. This area is an ideal 'icebreaker' for those arriving, enabling them to meet their fellow guests informally and later for exchange of thoughts and ideas over coffee, or even something a little stronger.

On the subject of alcohol it has become something of a tradition to create the occasional 'special cocktail' for certain groups. For instance when a 'Chocolate Evening' was held to raise funds for Charlton Church, the cocktail contained a mixture of Brandy, Port, Grand Marnier, egg yolks, sugar, nutmeg and ice, apparently this mixture *will* taste of chocolate. Another concoction was made for a group of ordinands, called 'A Vickers Lot' (Peter and Mary Vickers being members of the retreat). It consisted of a mixture of Vodka, Marascino, Blue Curaçao, grapefruit juice and ice!

Ever since the time of Diana Day, the Companions, a group of young people from Croxley Green in Hertfordshire, have been coming with Michael Hart to Holland House on retreat and have also helped with special events, often in costume, such as a Victorian breakfast and numerous festivals, one in Elizabethan dress.

The underlying theme of Peter's time at Holland House has been imaginative diversification. There has been a shift from purely a retreat house to something that has encompassed a wide spectrum of events and conferences, putting a greater emphasis on formation of the laity. There are still retreats and parish weekends but also study courses, evening meetings, dinners and special events. The joy is that all this has been achieved without in any way losing that special atmosphere and sense of peace that has always been so important a part of the House since its inception.

So much has taken place at Holland House that it is hardly possible to give a complete picture of all that has happened in the past eleven years. However, a flavour of that period can be given by reference to the programmes that have been compiled. For the first few years of his Wardenship, Peter Middlemiss was looking for opportunities to develop the work in the Diocese of Worcester, gently broadening the work and scope of the house. Then he was reaching out to other denominations of the wider Christian Church, as well as exploring new developments in themed retreats, and various courses on personality type.

By 1989 the programme included such diverse items as an evening concert by the Laetare Singers, a concert by mezzo-soprano Anna Jones singing songs by Purcell, Schubert, Mozart and Handel, and a weekend of meditation and contemplation conducted by the Revd Canon Dr Norman Todd, who was incidentally paying his fourth visit to Holland House. A Roman Catholic sister, from the Order of the Holy Child Jesus, gave a three-day session on *Personal and Spiritual Growth Through Journalling* and, in December of that year, Clare Freeman conducted a weekend group on *Making Career and Life Decisions*. There were also clergy Quiet Days and several *Myers Briggs Workshops*, helping participants to relate their personality type to their spirituality of ministry.

In May of the following year, 1990, a week-long pilgrimage to Iona was undertaken by the Friends, and this remains one of the highlights of the life of Holland House. This first pilgrimage was followed four years later by an equally memorable pilgrimage to Lindisfarne.

1990 was to see another change at Holland House. For the past seven years, Peter had been running the house with the help of the regular staff and young assistants who usually came for about twelve months after completing their studies. (It may in passing noted that a number of the assistants subsequently went on to train for full-time ministry.) However, the work was developing and, if opportunities were to be explored, a more permanent deputy would be needed.

At about the time that this was under consideration, Peter was organising The Association of Laity Centres annual conference at Hengrave Hall, Suffolk, a retreat centre run by Roman Catholic nuns. At this conference he was to meet William Swabey, a young Roman Catholic with a background in theology, teaching and business management. William had written to Peter some time before, asking about the possibilities of conference-centre work: and at Peter's suggestion William attended the Suffolk event. The outcome of this meeting was that William, and his wife Rosemary, came to Holland House, where he was able to use both his theology and business training in a creative context where they would both be useful.

As Deputy Warden at Holland House, William was able to bring, as well as his faith and business training, his recent knowledge of, and contacts with, the academic world. This has assisted greatly in the development of theology courses, particularly those run in conjunction with Birmingham University.

In addition to this work, William completed a Master's Degree in Adult Education, the final study of which concentrated on the implications of the thoughts of the Swiss theologian Hans Urs von Balthasar for Adult Christian formation in a church-world setting. The initial research for this took him to Germany to interview Academy staff on their methods in the Protestant Academy of Bad Boll, near Stuttgart, and the Catholic Academy of Freiburg. Thus in September 1994 the first one-year theology course at Holland House, *Modern Theological Approaches*, was pioneered.

In the autumn of 1990, Peter was elected to the General Synod of the Church of England. Along with this came the opportunity to enter more fully into national and international networks, to which an understanding of the purpose and potential of residential resource centres could be usefully contributed. In November 1993 he was a prime mover in founding ARCHWAY, the Anglican Retreat and Conference

House Wardens' Association. Its first conference was held at Holland House.

In 1989 the Baptist Union Retreat Group, BURG, gave the first ever Baptist Union retreat in Britain. This was not the first visit to Holland House by Baptists but the first held by BURG. One of those attending, Paul Tucker from King's Langley, wrote later in an issue of *Vision Magazine* dated 1990:

> To be still and listen to the voice of God is at the heart of the retreat movement, to come away from the noise and frenzied activity of the world and simply to 'be'. To do this is not easy, and the right environment is necessary to heighten the senses to the beauty of God. Such a place is Holland House, a retreat centre in the heart of the village of Cropthorne.

The sense of 'togetherness with God' was surely increased by the visits of Rabbi Dr Norman Soloman. The Rabbi has made two visits to Holland House, each time with his wife Devora. The first, in 1990, was a three-day course for the Gloucester School of Ministry, when they joined with the staff of the Centre for the Study of Judaism and Jewish Christian Relations. The second visit (1992) was for a 'Day of Reflection', with the title, *Judaism a Living Faith*. To quote the Rabbi:

> The relaxed and peaceful surroundings generated a feeling of openness and trust amongst participants; we were able to face and acknowledge the past bitterness of relations between Jews and Christians, whilst feeling at one with ourselves and confident in our shared witness to the contemporary world.

A gift to the House from a member of the 'Friends' has enabled those visiting to enjoy to an even greater extent the peace and tranquillity of the gardens. In 1994 a Retreat Hut was given to the 'Friends' and erected on the lawns where they slope to the river. Visitors are able to look across the Avon towards the Lenches, which are sometimes softly blue and hazy, at other times vividly clear, the sun shining on their slopes showing every detail.

Ecumenism, Art, Spirituality, and Still More

In the last few years so much has developed at Holland House that it is difficult to give little more than a flavour of all the activities by listing just one or two of the highlights. With Peter wanting to stress the international aspect of the work, it was a happy day when Holland House was able to celebrate becoming a full member of the European Association of Academies and Laity Centres, which Peter and william attended in Spain in the summer of 1993. Membership was also reflected in the new title of the house, namely *Holland House, Retreat, Conference and Laity Centre*.

Another highlight, with an ecumenical flavour , was the celebration of the diamond jubilee of his ordination by Monsignor James Crichton. Mgr Crichton had recently been honoured by Rome with the award of an Honorary Doctorate of Liturgy, a subject that he had studied, lectured on and written about all his priestly life. For the last 22 years he had been parish priest in Pershore, a great change from his travels, which had taken him all over the world.

The celebration was held at Holland House as part of the summer gathering of the Society of St Gregory, a society of which Mgr Crichton had been, to quote the chairman writing in the society's publication *Music and Liturgy*, '... a pioneering member.... He was part of the movement that spearheaded the development of the liturgy in the early days.'

Not long after this special event Mgr. Crichton was invited back again, this time to a dinner hosted by the Church of England Liturgical Commission. On this occasion he distinguished himself further by taking no notice whatever of the kitchen staff whose efforts to stop him smoking in the dining room were to no avail!

As an indication of the way in which the breadth of the programme was developing, one can only cite as fairly typical some of the events held in the months of August and September 1994.

In August a five-day painting holiday was led by Colin Jones: this was followed by a week-long session on *Painting and Prayer*, which already had a waiting list when the brochure was published. Later in the month, a weekend of meditation and contemplation was led by Revd Canon Dr Norman Todd. As well as another concert by the very popular Laetare Singers, the September programme included *ARCIC (Anglican – Roman Catholic International Commission) thus far*, and a Laity Festival with workshops, theatre, celebrations.

Art has been important in the work of the house. On several occasions there have been retreats combining art and prayer, as in an early programme in 1991 when Sue Waldron Skinner and the Revd Charles Shells gave a five day course in *Painting and Prayer*. Earlier in the same year, the Revd Robert Cooper gave a weekend retreat entitled *Calligraphy Retreat*. For many years during August, the Malvern artist Aubrey Phillips has also run painting courses at Holland House, and exhibitions of contemporary art have also been part of the life of the house. Over the last few years the Warden has made a collection of contemporary prints which often prove to be the stimulus for interesting conversations.

Spirituality has not been ignored, as can be seen by programme items such as two days given to *Ignatian Spirituality* (1992), *An Introduction to the Institute of Contemporary Spirituality* (1990), *A Benedictine Experience* (1993) and *Spirituality and Vocation* a two-day retreat especially for women, led by Dr Una Kroll. These are but the merest taste of what has been on offer at Holland House over the years.

Nor has the house been isolated from those around it in the village. Always in the programme is the May *Cropthorne Walkabout*, when many gardens in the village are open, and

luncheons and teas are served at Holland House. To quote
Mrs Blizard again:

> When Deaconess Mayes was running the house we all felt
> part of it and it felt part of the village. That was rather lost
> when the Deaconess went, but we have got it back since
> Peter came.

The 'Friends' have always been fortunate in their chairmen.
Over the past ten years, first Daphne Pagnamenta, and then
the retired Bishop of Oxford, the Rt Revd Kenneth Wool-
combe have held this office. During those ten years they
increased membership of the 'Friends' from 100 to 500. As
well as being strongly supportive of all the 'Friends' worked
for and achieved, Daphne was also involved on an international scale with Riding for the Disabled. After her death
which, sadly, was only shortly after she gave up the office of
chairman, a section of the rose garden was dedicated to her
memory. During the Bishop's term of office a series of Theological Dinners was instituted which have proved to be of
great interest. Held in a very informal manner, attended by
about fifteen or sixteen people on average, the speaker dines
with the guests and then gives his paper whilst all remain
seated at the table, together with their glass of wine. Formal-
ity is dispensed with and questions usually become a fairly
general discussion. These dinners are of great interest to
both professional theologians and those who merely take a
scholarly interest in the subject.

The speakers are very varied, including in 1995 the Revd
Peter King, a Baptist, who spoke on *The Dark Night: A Contem-
plation of Bonhoeffer and Merton*. Other speakers have included
David Moss on *Baptism: an Allegory*, Peter Bristow on *Christi-
anity and Politics*, and Dr Gareth Jones on *Demythologising
Bultman*.

The same format ensures the success of meetings of the
Monday Matters Network, when participants discuss issues
concerning faith and life, especially in the area of members'
work or main activity; and the *Books Network*, when local

authors come to talk about their latest book. Reading parties connected to the Books Network have yielded a number of reviews published in *Reviews in Religion and Theology*. The combination of good food and interesting conversation before a stimulating talk, followed by general discussion is almost irresistible.

The tradition of good meals, which Diana aimed for at Holland House was continued by Sarah Bennett until her marriage in 1989. Since then, the tradition has been more than ably carried on by Linda Campbell; she cooks, serves and smiles, and is a very vital part of the present team. In running the kitchen she is also always aware of the main purpose of the house.

There have of course been humorous happenings at Holland House, disasters did not happen only in the early days. In the winter of 1986, when the weather was very severe and there was thick snow on the ground, all the power failed and it was back to the days of the Old House in the 1940s. The problem lay not only in coping with finding candles to light the house, and searching for wood for the fires, but much of the food was in deep-freezes, not in use in the 1940s' kitchens of the *Old House*. After a day or two with no power, the temperature within the cabinets was beginning to rise, so what should be done? Someone had a bright idea: the sunken garden was full of snow, 'Let's *bury* all the frozen food before it begins to thaw'. There was much hilarity as first the food was buried (shades of Diana and the dried vegetables down the well), then of course it later had to be found and identified for use. Cries of 'Where are the peas?' and 'Where did we bury the stewing steak?' could be heard as the cooks attempted to locate a 'balanced' meal.

A happily humorous occasion was when in 1987 David Moss, who had worked at the house as an assistant, got married. The marriage ceremony was at Cropthorne Church, and the reception was held at Holland House. After the reception, the happy couple walked with their parents and

guests down to the car park. The guests stopped when they
reached what they thought was the honeymoon car, but the
bride and groom just kept on walking, right down to the river
bank. There, hidden and waiting for them, was a boat to take
them on the first short stage of their honeymoon trip. The
groom's mother was said to have taken some time to recover
from the unexpectedly romantic departure of the newly-
weds.

International Contacts and Friendship

Bearing in mind the postwar origins of such centres across
Europe and beyond, it can be seen why one of the ambitions
of Peter Middlemiss was to broaden the contacts of Holland
House in order to give it an overseas dimension. In this he
has succeeded in several ways.

In 1993 Ulrike Poppe, of the Berlin/Brandenburg Academy
visited Cropthorne during the week of prayer for Christian
Unity. She was invited to attend services in the area to speak
of 'The Church in Germany Today'. She was able to tell her
listeners of Life and faith in Germany before and after the
Berlin Wall came down.

Dr Fritz Erich Anhelm, until recently General Secretary of
the European Association of Academies & Laity Centres, has
also visited and given talks at Holland House, the House now
being a member of the Association.

For the last few years, parties of Americans have visited
Cropthorne, staying at Holland House and exploring the
countryside, towns and theatres in the locality. The organisation through which they come is based in America and
called Elder Hostel. The week at Holland House could be
described as 'Alternative tourism with an ecumenical flavour'. To ensure that the American visitors get a real 'flavour'
of English life and hospitality, their trips are not by coach but
by individual members of the 'Friends' taking three or four
of the visitors out in their own cars, either on a formal

planned visit such as to the theatre, or on journeys around the Cotswolds and Vale of Evesham towns and villages.

Staffing at Holland House has for the last few years also been very international. Young people come from many countries, including Hungary, Czechoslovakia, Italy and Germany, to work for just a few months in the summer, or sometimes for a whole year, to improve their English or to experience foreign travel and work. In 1994 the Revd Ejike Okoro, a Methodist minister from Nigeria, stayed at the house for four months as a member of staff, visiting local Methodist churches. The Methodist Central Division of Ministries also makes use of Holland House; all this is a further example of the ecumenical and international relationships built up over the years.

It is interesting to recall in this context that one of the first members of staff in the original *Old House* was a young Catholic from Italy — a full circle of ecumenical and overseas friendship after fifty years!

The day-to-day work of the house has now for many years included the accommodation of a wide variety of groups, courses and conferences which, while not necessarily church-based, have contributed to the breadth of its vision. These have included groups training in counselling skills, stress management, dealing with drink-related problems, HIV, and death and bereavement. Among some of the better-known organisations that have used the house over recent years are NACRO, MENCAP, Barnado's, Cheshire Homes, Oxfam, Christian Aid, and the Council for the Protection of Rural England.

In 1992, a particularly good year, the house achieved over 5,000 'bed-nights' for the first time in its history. To mark this achievement, all staff members were presented with glasses engraved with the portrait of Mrs Holland and the total number of bednights namely 5,175.

It is impossible to list all the Church groups that have stayed in and benefited from the house in recent years.

However, quickly leafing through the House diary reveals that besides parish groups, others such as the West of England Ministerial Training Course (formerly the Gloucester School of Ministry), Bishop's conferences for the Dioceses of Worcester and Lichfield, young priests' retreat for the Archdiocese of Birmingham, and the Aston Training Scheme. Groups of Methodist youth workers have stayed as has the Social Welfare Commission of the Roman Catholic Bishops' Conference, a group of Unitarian Ministers, a Lutheran Church visit from Stuttgart, and so the list goes on... and will surely continue to grow.

Such a history will never, God willing, have an end. So perhaps to give a lighthearted finish to the story of Holland House so far one can quote the comment written in the visitors' book — a quote which is to appear on the latest edition of the Holland House Chocolates:

Holland House puts the *treat* back into retreat.

Officers

Mr Herbert Chiswell Jones
Mr Roy Roberts
Mrs Jan Wilson

Past Trustees

The Ven. Robin Bennett
The Ven. Peter Coleman
The Rt Revd Tony Dumper
Mrs Henrietta Woods

Bibliography

Cropthorne Camera of Minnie Holland, C.D. and G.H. Webb,
   E.R. Cornell (copyright dated 1978).
Diocesan Archives, re. Holland House, in possession of the
   Worcester Diocesan Registrar, M.G. Huskinson.
Holland House Archives.
Personal correspondence to the author from various sources
   (now held at Holland House).
Report of Bishop's Working Party, 1974. CRO, Worcester.
Victoria County History, Worcester, Vol. 3.